Alcohol education

Alcohol education
A handbook for health and welfare professionals

Barbara Howe

R

Tavistock/Routledge
London and New York

First published 1989 by Routledge
11 New Fetter Lane, London EC4P 4EE
29 West 35th Street, New York, NY 10001

© 1989 Barbara Howe

Phototypeset in 10pt Times by
Mews Photosetting, Beckenham, Kent
Printed and bound in Great Britain by
Mackays of Chatham PLC, Chatham, Kent

British Library Cataloguing in Publication Data

Howe, Barbara
    Alcohol education: a handbook for health and
    welfare professionals.
    1. Great Britain. Alcohol education
    I. Title
    362.2'9286

    ISBN 0-415-01890-0 ISBN 0-415-01891-9 (pbk.)

Library of Congress Cataloging-in-Publication Data

Howe, Barbara, 1955–
    Alcohol education : a handbook for health and welfare
    professionals / by Barbara Howe.
        p. cm.
    Bibliography: p.
    Includes index.
    1. Alcoholism — Study and teaching. 2. Social work with
alcoholics. I. Title.
HV125.H68 1989
362.2'92–dc19   88-29743
                                                              CIP
ISBN 0-415-01890-0. ISBN 0-415-01891-9 (pbk.)

Education is only a ladder to gather fruit from the tree of knowledge, not the fruit itself.

Anon

Contents

Contents

Foreword

Alcohol is drunk and enjoyed by most people in society. Its taste, the ambience of its main sales points (restaurants, pubs and parties), the expression of 'sharing' implied in mutual buying of drinks, the 'excuse' to attend social gatherings — all help explain its popularity. But good soft drinks *could* satisfy most of these needs. Alcohol's difference is its mood-altering properties which are greatly sought after and enjoyed by most drinkers.

Thus its capacity to encourage relaxation, reduce inhibition, promote sociability, relieve stress and obtain, in varying — largely chosen-degrees, inebriation and loss of control/consciousness is greatly valued in society. It is a welcome drug.

However, as a society, we have got its use wrong, as has been recognised for years by alcohol abuse agencies, the probation service and churches, who 'pick up the pieces'. Those who drink too much — or at the wrong times — damage not only their health, and often their careers, but the happiness and wellbeing of family, colleagues and friends.

Now, those helping problem drinkers are less alone in recognising the other side of the coin. The proportion of the public perceiving alcohol problems as 'serious' has risen from 26% to 43% over the past ten years. Similar shifts in awareness are seen in the USSR, the USA (where the legal drinking age was actually raised in most states), in Scandinavia and Australia.

The UK government has now followed that trend. It set up, in 1987, a high-level Ministerial Group on Alcohol Abuse. The Home Office has acknowledged links between alcohol and crime and the DHSS has urged local and health authorities to put alcohol further up their list of priorities.

This welcome — if belated — response will now devolve heavily onto health and welfare professionals. Their role will be critical.

Firstly, because any strategy for reducing alcohol misuse depends on knowledgeable planners and professionals. Secondly because, so often, the health and welfare staff are 'in the right place at the right time'. They see clients in their own homes, or in relaxed encounters where 'drink' is not top of the discussion topics — and thus may be approached more easily. They see, often early on, the telltale signs of excessive drinking — family, financial, emotional, work or health problems. Thirdly, because they can build an ongoing relationship of trust with the drinker and the family — vital to successful intervention.

Indeed, most problem drinkers who receive any help or advice will get this not from a specialist alcohol service, but from generic professionals.

The problem, however, is that alcohol education — both about prevention (promoting 'safer drinking') and about intervention and help — is in a poor state. It is underfunded and professionally has been unrecognised.

Training organisations for professional workers are slow to accord alcohol education the prominent place it merits on their training schedules. Medical education almost ignores alcohol use and abuse. Elsewhere, attention to this major area is scanty.

This book seeks to plug that gap. Barbara Howe's book is aimed at health and welfare professionals. However, so good is it that virtually every reader can learn from it, from the generalist to the alcohol specialist. Many of the tips — for example on listening techniques — go beyond just alcohol and will enhance the skills of many professionals.

The eyes of many will be on health and welfare professionals to play their part in helping problem drinkers. This handbook should give them the knowledge, the skills and the confidence to respond.

Dianne Hayter
Alcohol Concern
London, September 1988

Preface

The aim of this book is to provide a practical, easy-to-read guide for health and welfare professionals who are keen to develop the alcohol education aspects of their work and enable their clients and patients to use alcohol in a harm-free way. Some professional workers avoid becoming involved in alcohol education because they feel it is an area that requires specialist knowledge, skills, and techniques, that it is time-consuming, and that, above all, it is not especially effective. It seems much easier to leave clients and patients with a leaflet on alcohol abuse and some well-intended advice, rather than working out the possible place and role of alcohol education in any given intervention.

This book explores some of those feelings by considering a range of problems associated with inappropriate drinking, the effects on individuals, families, and the wider community, and the range of educational responses open to workers. Alcohol education *can* and *should* be a central part of clinical and casework activity and can be seen as a caring activity. The text develops principles about alcohol education on which to base good practice and, by including a series of practical exercises for use with individuals and families, aims to increase professionals' confidence and competence in broaching the subject of alcohol.

The subject matter should interest all those whose day-to-day work may bring them into contact with people experiencing various degrees of alcohol and alcohol-related problems. These could range from severe alcohol dependence and its associated health problems through to legal, financial, employment, or marital difficulties. The text is divided into three sections — getting alcohol education into context, getting down to it, and getting over difficulties. A glossary of terms and a recommended reading list have also been included for readers' information and convenience.

Acknowledgements

While writing this book, I was fortunate to receive help and support from many friends and colleagues and I should like to offer them my thanks and appreciation.

Thanks are due to all those who took an interest, but especially to the people who read the manuscript critically and provided me with suggestions for improvements. They include Mary Dobson, a nurse specialist in psychotherapy, Dr Robin Means, a research fellow, Jane Randell, a health education and training consultant, and Linda Wright, a lecturer in health education. I am grateful to Dianne Hayter who is the Director of Alcohol Concern for writing the foreword and for her interest in this publication. I am also indebted to the Research Committee of the School of Education at the University of Durham for the financial assistance it provided and to colleagues from the Northern Regional Health Authority for their support and encouragement.

Owing to a transition from one job to another during the writing phase, four different secretaries worked on the manuscript and I am deeply grateful to Janette Hill, Lynn Carrington, Margaret Gibson, and Cara McKenzie for the patience and care they showed in their work.

Every author depends on a good relationship with her publisher and my appreciation goes to Jo Campling, the series editor and Rosemary Nixon, the editor for Routledge for the interest and expertise they showed throughout the whole process.

Finally, and most importantly, I am grateful to Bob and my parents, Ann and Tom, for their faith in me.

Barbara Howe

Alcohol education:
getting it into context

Chapter one

Putting alcohol into context

A visitor from another planet could be forgiven for becoming rapidly confused about ambivalent, inconsistent attitudes towards alcohol and to its fluctuating role and position in our society. Over the centuries, the use of alcohol by the human race has been variously encouraged, condemned, manipulated, and prohibited and has led to great enjoyment and profit as well as misery and ruin. Today, society's response to alcohol is as ambivalent as ever and can be seen as a continuum on which punishment and prohibition lie at one end, treatment and rehabilitation near the middle, and education and training, often seen as the soft option, at the opposite end. The interplanetary visitor might also furrow his brow over the ever-changing labels given to those whose drinking behaviour is unacceptable to society and the multitude of pseudo-scientific explanations put forward to explain why some people drink happily throughout their lives whilst others get into difficulties. Clearly, the history of alcohol use presents a tangled web and it is worthwhile teasing out its various threads to set it in context, to learn lessons from the past, and to make informed predictions about the future.

The reasons why people use alcohol are as wide-ranging and varied as people themselves and it is worth noting our ingenuity in finding or inventing substances for ingestion that alter our state of consciousness. In the case of alcohol, the ingredients necessary to make it (water, sugar, yeast, and heat) were combined with a relatively simple fermentation process (yeast and sugary juice and heat) to introduce early, preliterate peoples to the effects of alcohol intoxication. Alcoholic drinks were well known to many early human civilizations and were used, not only for intoxication, but also in religious ceremonies where wine and beer were offered to the gods and became imbued with religious significance. Alcohol was familiar to the Egyptians, the ancient Hebrews, and the

Greeks and Romans, and both drinking and drunkenness are recurring themes in Greek and Roman mythology. Over-zealous attempts by religious devotees to alter their levels of consciousness by using alcohol meant that it fell particularly to religions to control such dangerous excesses. The prophet Isaiah complained: 'Priest and prophet are addicted to strong drink and bemused with wine; clamouring in their cups, confirmed topers, hiccuping in drunken stupor; every table is covered with vomit.' In the seventh century, Islam opted for total prohibition and the Koran condemned the use of wine. Such strong measures were repeated in Northern Europe and North America over 1,000 years later when some Protestant sects promoted abstinence from alcohol as one of the basic tenets of their religious beliefs. It is interesting to note how the more successful attempts to control alcohol misuse derive from a religious basis rather than from secular decree.

Religious disapproval apart, however, alcohol is now 'the chosen intoxicant of European peoples as it has been in many other parts of the world. It has been part of our lives from the very beginnings of our civilization and it is woven inextricably into our culture' (Special Committee of Royal College of Psychiatrists 1986:18). Today, consumption of alcohol increases worldwide as more countries become industrialized and as the alcohol industry itself develops into multinational companies (US Journal of Drug and Alcohol Dependence 1981:19). Since the turn of this century, various attempts have been made to control or prohibit the use of alcohol including the licensing laws introduced into Great Britain in 1915 and the policies of prohibition adopted in North America and Scandinavia in the 1920s. Such stringent measures gave rise to many problems of their own and there are calls today, in Great Britain at least, to extend licensing hours and adopt what is seen as a more relaxed, continental approach to the use of alcohol. The visitor from space might conclude that earthlings seem unable to make up their minds about alcohol. We appear to want all the benefits and pleasures alcohol may bring and we accord alcohol a special place in society, yet we remain unconvinced about the type of measures (if any) that should be taken to control our consumption of alcohol and to limit its potential for harm.

Why drink? Why continue to drink?

If a cross-section of people, both those who have alcohol problems and those who do not, were asked why they drink, their responses would include some of the following:

to relax	to enjoy myself
to socialize	to help me to sleep
to celebrate	to reward myself
to forget my worries	to refresh me
to relieve boredom	to enhance a meal

Society appears to have found reasons for using alcohol on almost every occasion to relieve or heighten almost all emotional or psychological states. If feeling low, we drink 'to cheer outselves up'. If tired, we imagine that alcohol will 'pep us up' and yet we also use it to help us relax, to wind down at the end of the day, and to get off to sleep. We use alcohol to enhance food at mealtimes and yet alcohol has also (mistakenly) been seen as a food in itself so that we joke about having 'a liquid lunch'. (See Chapter 3, Myths and misunderstandings about alcohol.)

Further analysis of our apparent reasons for drinking reveals that there may be deeper reasons that we find difficult to recognize or express. These include the desire to protect ourselves from feelings of inadequacy, depression, tension, or loneliness, and to avoid confrontation (with parents, spouse, colleagues) and emotional trauma. For a short space of time, alcohol can alleviate these feelings and may help us to feel better about ourselves and more in control of our own lives. As the effects of alcohol wear off, however, so does the short-term respite and we are left with the discomfort provoked by the original problem plus any additional mental and physical discomforts brought on by over-indulgence in alcohol. At this stage, some people will use alcohol again to make the problem retreat and to relieve a hangover or mild depression following a bout of drinking. This can lead to the vicious circle of relief drinking, in which each drink is taken in the hope that it will stave off any apparent or potential ill-effects caused by the previous one.

Why can one person use alcohol to its best advantage gaining pleasure and enjoyment from it, whereas another person, in similar circumstances, gets into difficulties and experiences one or more problems as a result of drinking? In his chapter on the causes of alcoholism, Anthony Clare comments on some of the major models put forward to explain this phenomenon but warns that:

> many attempts to provide such an explanation have been made
> but to date no single explanatory theory has proven adequate.
> Indeed, partly as a consequence of this failure, many experts

subscribe to the view that there is no single cause and that alcoholism is best envisaged as a condition in which several causal factors operate to produce the final clinical picture.

(Clare 1979:64–76)

The major theories lay particular emphasis on one of three factors: biological, psychological, or socio-cultural, although the drug properties of alcohol, the constitution and personality of the individual consuming it, and the context in which the drinking takes place must also be acknowledged.

Biological causes

Focusing on the pharmacological properties of alcohol, the biological model of alcohol dependence highlights biochemical, physiological, and neurophysiological abnormalities. It looks closely at an individual's tolerance to alcohol, whether he experiences withdrawal symptoms and a craving to drink when alcohol is absent and whether there has been a loss of control over consumption. The bulk of research that supports this model however, has been carried out on people who are severely dependent on alcohol and, although there is a lot of evidence of disturbances in physical functioning, the *cause* of such disturbances is not clear.

Other research has considered whether individuals who are physically dependent on alcohol possess some metabolic or genetic defect that renders them particularly vulnerable to developing drinking problems. Metabolic studies have shown that 'alcohol exercises a "normalizing" effect in alcoholics' but have not proved that this condition precedes their dependence on alcohol. Reasons for suspecting genetic factors can be argued more strongly in that some studies have shown that rates of alcoholism are higher among the relatives of alcoholics than in the general population. Others argue, however, that alcoholism is too complex a behaviour pattern to be explained simply by genetic causes. There are arguments both for and against this explanation, although the case has yet to be proven.

Psychological causes

The psychological model is based on the idea of the 'alcoholic personality' — a person who is both vulnerable and predisposed to developing alcohol problems. Derived from classic psychoanalytical theory, the model views alcohol dependence as a result of failure in the personality development of the drinker who uses alcohol as a means of coping with emotional conflicts. Almost considering alcoholism as a psychiatric illness, the model does not explain why other individuals, who also show signs of immature emotional functioning, psychiatric illness, and deviant behaviour, do not go on to develop alcohol problems.

The personality theory of alcoholism similarly looks for a consistent set of personality traits that might indicate a 'dependent personality'. No specific traits have been found, however, (such as high anxiety levels, low self-esteem, or inferiority), that can be proved always to *precede* the development of alcohol problems rather than arising *as a result of* their development. A further psychological theory is based on behavioural principles and sees alcoholism as a pattern of behaviour that can be both learned and unlearned. If an individual learns that drinking alcohol can reduce tension and anxiety, the drinking behaviour becomes reinforced. Whenever tense or anxious, he uses alcohol and gains relief as a result of its pharmacological properties. Continued drinking, however, can have adverse effects and the drinker may find that the pharmacological properties of alcohol, because of their addictive nature, themselves create stress and anxiety, which can only be relieved by further drinking. Support for this theory comes mainly from animal studies that have not taken into account human reinforcers such as parental habits or peer-group pressure.

Other theorists have drawn on concepts used in transactional analysis (see Chapters 3 and 8) to see alcoholism as a game in which a series of transactions takes place between individuals with the purpose of obtaining some personal reward or advantage. Such rewards or 'payoffs' might include gaining attention, avoiding emotional deficiencies within a relationship, or coercing others (by threatening self-damage) to offer care and support.

Socio-cultural causes

This model moves away from the individual's biochemistry and psychopathology to consider social and environmental factors that might influence alcohol consumption. Occupational factors appear to be important as certain occupations (barman, managing director, seaman, salesman, journalist, and doctor) are associated with significantly higher rates of alcoholism than others. This appears to be associated with the availability of alcohol, the lack of work supervision, stress, and separation from normal social and sexual relationships. Again, there is little evidence to prove that these work circumstances are the *cause* of alcohol problems rather than that they are particularly sought by the individual.

Ethnic factors suggest that alcohol use and misuse is controlled, to some extent, by underlying attitudes to alcohol and the drinking practices of various ethnic groups. For example, there are low rates of alcoholism among Jews, Mormons, and Moslems due, according to the theory, to their cultural prohibition of the use or misuse of alcohol. Other countries, such as Ireland, Scotland, and the United States are seen as having ambivalent attitudes towards alcohol use and misuse and associated high rates of alcohol problems. Clare 1979 says 'they oscillate between a permissive tolerance of drunkenness and a moral denunciation of physiological dependence' (p. 73).

Socio-cultural models also look at familial factors, and studies in Sweden, Switzerland, and the United States have shown that higher rates of alcoholism exist in the parents and/or siblings of alcoholics than in the general population. This could indicate that family behaviour patterns are influential in the development of alcohol problems or that parental disagreement about drinking and ambivalent attitudes and punitiveness with regard to drinking practices give rise to environmental stress that provokes or precipitates episodes of alcohol misuse.

It is likely that each theory holds a grain of truth but that no single theory can be seen as the sole cause of drinking problems. Clare concludes his chapter by saying:

> with a simple disease model of alcoholism which envisages the cause of alcoholism as an organically based defect rendering the alcoholic vulnerable to alcohol, the therapeutic solution is a strict adherence to an abstinence regime pending some medical breakthrough aimed at remedying the effect. A view of alcoholism as learned maladaptive behaviour, on the other hand, holds out the possibility of retraining some alcoholics to drink socially and responsibly. An emphasis on socio-cultural causation directs attention to such factors as the availability of alcohol in society, its advertising, marketing and retailing, the societal value placed on its consumption, the manner in which alcohol use is imitated and maintained, the relative cost of the substance and the legal controls on its use and abuse. It seems clear that a proper and comprehensive approach to the treatment of

alcoholism needs to reflect the multifactorial approach that is now implicit in current theories of causation advanced by most theorists in this area.

(Clare 1979)

To understand how such perspectives have arisen and how they, and other factors, shape our attitudes to alcohol and our drinking behaviour, it is helpful to go right back to the beginning and look at how we learned about alcohol and to identify the influences that were at work along the way.

Process of socialization

Few of us can pinpoint with accuracy the very first time we tasted alcohol, but we can usually remember our early feelings towards it and our

Table 1.1 Learning about alcohol through a process of socialization

Life stage	Potential influences	Constant influences
Birth	socio-cultural background parents family	availability price legislation
Early childhood	friends and their families school teachers older brothers and sisters	
Teens	own experiences parties, discos peer-group influences training college work own income greater autonomy	
20s — 40s	marriage long-term relationships children changing life style	
Middle age	responsibility for others divorce or separation bereavement income fluctuation unemployment or redundancy	
Old age	retirement ill-health loneliness	

subsequent reactions. For many people, their first introduction to alcohol took place within the family setting, perhaps at a wedding, at a party, or at Christmas and may have provoked feelings of curiosity, excitement, happiness, and anticipation. For certain people, their first taste of alcohol was an outright disappointment that left them wondering why adults make such a fuss about it. Some may have enjoyed the dizziness or lightheadedness that ensued, whilst others disliked feeling out of control or suffered unpleasant after-effects. Whether their first reaction to alcohol was positive or negative, most people continue to use alcohol to some extent and, by a series of experiments, 'learn' to use it to its best advantage. Such experiments — trying out different drinks and varying measures, mixing drinks, getting intoxicated, and experiencing hangovers — usually take place during adolescence and will also be influenced by other factors, including parental attitudes, availability, fashion, peer-group influences, and advertising (see Table 1.1).

Influences identified at each separate life stage in Table 1.1 will not necessarily stop as we move on to the next stage, but may continue to affect us for the rest of our lives.

Why change and how?

Nobody deliberately starts out in life intending to become a problem drinker and yet many people, at some stage in their lives, get into difficulties with their drinking. Few of us receive any factual education — either formally or informally — about alcohol and how to use it sensibly. Our attitudes are shaped by a variety of influences and we are presented with conflicting images of alcohol put forward by doctors, the licensed trade, the media, the police, and advertising. It is because of this welter of conflicting images, of the very real potential of alcohol to cause harm and our imperfect understanding of the facts, that we should be prepared to consider changing our attitudes towards alcohol and possibly amending our behaviour. Psychologists tell us that we are most likely to repeat forms of behaviour that bring us personal rewards and also attract social approval. Drinking alcohol can achieve both of these as the drug effect gives us a fairly rapid, personal reward and drinking itself is seen as a sociable, amiable activity that merits society's approval. This rosy view of alcohol, however, should be tempered by the recognition that society can equally reject, despise, or denigrate the drinker whose behaviour has become unacceptable. Few people wish to be treated in this way and yet, often, their dependence on alcohol is so necessary to them that they continue to risk censure and rejection rather than altering their behaviour.

It is a mistake to believe that people who experience difficulties with their drinking will inevitably pursue a slippery descent into ruin and oblivion. It is more helpful to consider drinking in terms of a continuum where alcohol consumption may increase in response to a changed life style, a major life event such as divorce or increased stress at work or *may equally decline* in response to the same circumstances. An individual's drinking behaviour can and will change but this often requires a raised awareness of the pros and cons of alcohol use and a careful examination of how they affect not only the individual but also the wider community and society in which he lives. At the same time, we should be wary of concentrating only on the problems that may arise from alcohol use and should acknowledge that there are many benefits associated with drinking and that the majority of people who use alcohol do so in a non-harmful way.

The role of alcohol — in society, in the community, at home

Were alcohol to be discovered for the first time today, it would probably be labelled as a poison and relegated to the pharmacists' shelves. Alcohol is a legal, psychotropic drug capable of damaging living tissue or even killing a living organism and yet it is accorded a special role in some of society's most respected, treasured ceremonies and rituals. If we consider the life span of an ordinary individual, we can see how and where alcohol plays a part and appreciate how drinking is a normal, accepted part of many people's lives (see Table 1.2).

Alcohol is used in solemn ceremonies to mark important occasions, to cap achievements, and to seal contracts and is also an integral part of many happy celebrations to indicate hospitality and to ease the process of socializing among families and friends. There are many occasions on which it is traditional to drink alcohol, for example, at Christmas or at a party — and several occasions on which heavy drinking is expected such as at stag parties or New Year's Eve parties. As among earlier civilizations, alcohol is used today as part of several initiation ceremonies into adulthood, the married status, a new job, a new sports club, or a new life style. It smoothes periods of transition and is used as a reward and a mark of success. On a more personal level, alcohol is also used to ease the transition from 'work time' to 'leisure time'. As our lives become more and more compartmentalized, it becomes increasingly

Table 1.2 Use of alcohol throughout one life span

Life event	Use of alcohol
Tom Green is born	At the christening to 'wet the baby's head' and welcome him into the world
Tom teaches the age of majority	To celebrate his attaining voting age, traditional to get extremely intoxicated
Tom gets engaged	Engagement party to seal the contract and to celebrate the happy occasion. Pre-wedding celebrations, stag and hen party
Tom gets married	A toast to the bridal couple to wish them health, wealth, and happiness
Tom receives promotion	To celebrate, let off steam and anticipate an improved standard of living
Tom and his wife have a baby	Tom traditionally celebrates the newborn's arrival with male friends, also at the christening
Tom is made redundant	To cope with emotional stress, frustration, boredom, unaccustomed, unstructured time
Tom and his wife reach 60th wedding anniversary	A large family party to mark this milestone in the couple's life
Tom's wife dies	To salve his grief, as a crutch, to ward off loneliness
Tom dies	Alcohol used at the funeral as a mark of hospitality to fortify grieving relatives, and to give Tom 'a good send-off'

difficult to switch off from work quickly and make the most of our relaxation and leisure time. Alcohol is an asset on such occasions as, at the end of a morning's or afternoon's work, the very act of consuming alcohol usually necessitates a change of environment, pace, and company. Combined with the relaxing, de-stressing effects of alcohol itself, we are helped to move smoothly from a work situation into a leisure situation. For example, the factory workers have a couple of beers or lagers at lunchtime, the office workers call in for a couple of gin and tonics or glasses of wine on their way home from work, or the executives have aperitifs and a few glasses of wine with their evening meals.

Even among moderate drinkers however, the positive payoffs

derived from drinking may be balanced by one or two negative payoffs as shown in Table 1.3.

Table 1.3 Hypothetical balance sheet of a moderate drinker

| | Payoffs from drinking | |
	Positive	Negative
Feelings	'High' stimulated after a few drinks	Headache, dry mouth and mildly depressed next morning if drunk a lot
Performance	Increased energy and motivation immediately after lunch	Reduced concentration at work in afternoon if drinks at lunchtime
Relationships with others	Closer, less tense with work colleagues	
Economic		Leaves money short at weekend if drinks a lot Friday night
Others	Part of enjoyable relaxation at snooker club and at home with family and friends	

Source: Robertson, I., Hodgson, R., Orford, J. *et al.* (1984).

In the case of heavy drinkers, the negative payoffs become more pronounced and the likelihood of experiencing medical, legal, or social problems increases (see Table 1.4). From an educational perspective, it is helpful to visualize (and to help the drinker visualize) heavy drinking in terms of both positive and negative payoffs and to remember that drinking alcohol is rarely a totally positive or a totally negative experience. For most people it is usually a mixture of both and the secret lies in finding the right balance. Due to a lack of education about alcohol — either formal or informal — many drinkers find it easy to list the immediate benefits of alcohol but more difficult to assess the mid- and long-term drawbacks. If heavy drinking becomes normal practice for an individual, it may take the intervention of a professional (doctor, policeman, social worker) to highlight the fact that the negative payoffs from drinking are outweighing the positive ones and may also be exacerbating current problems or creating new ones. If the mortality rate for excessive drinkers is approximately 2.5 times that for the ordinary population (NIAAA, *Information and Feature Service*, 1981:6), all people who drink should develop an appreciation of the types of problems that

Table 1.4 Hypothetical balance sheet of a heavy drinker

	Payoffs from drinking Positive	Negative
Feelings	Helps cope with family and job worries, relaxes	Feel guilty about drinking so much
Performance	Can face working after a few drinks	Making mistakes at work. One or two near misses in car
Relationships with family and friends	Meet several other heavy drinkers in local who are good company, able to assert myself	Family complaining not seeing me much, have embarrassed them a few times, they say I'm a changed character after drinking
Economic		Can't afford what spending on drink
Others		Put on a lot of weight

Source: Robertson, I., Hodgson, R., Orford, J., *et al.* (1984).

may arise as a result of inappropriate or exessive drinking.

Range of problems

It is virtually impossible to imagine individuals whose inappropriate level of drinking and subsequent problems affected only themselves and left untouched their wider community and society. Unless they lived a hermit-like life, it is probable that the drinking behaviour would affect several groups of people. In Figure 1.1, the drinker stands in the centre while the effects of his drinking ripple out through the family, the community, and society. A caring society, while trying to prevent alcohol problems on the one hand, must also be prepared to pay the costs involved in treatment and rehabilitation if it permits, and often condones, the use of alcohol.

Health problems caused by regular, heavy drinking may take time to develop and are sometimes overlooked or minimized by the drinker. The human body is able to withstand or adapt itself to the physiological effects of alcohol to such a degree that heavy drinkers may even be totally unaware of the damage they are causing themselves. Basically, 'alcohol is a depressant that acts as an anaesthetic on the central nervous system. It is absorbed unchanged into the stomach and small intestine and is

Figure 1.1 Wider effects of problem drinking

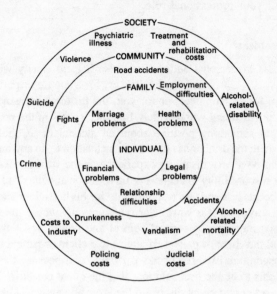

disseminated by the blood to all parts of the body, including the brain'. (Works 1974:7). Alcohol, therefore, has the potential to affect and harm all organs and tissues of the body. Cirrhosis of the liver is the physical problem most readily associated with alcohol although the brain, the heart, the digestive system, the kidneys, and the circulatory system may also be damaged by heavy drinking.

Professional perspectives

Health and welfare professionals tend to view alcohol and alcohol-related problems from differing perspectives; these are largely determined by their professional roles and what may represent an alcohol problem to the medical profession may not necessarily do so to the social-work profession. There are many different perspectives on alcohol problems — legal, social, economic, medical, environmental, political — that overlap from one profession to another so perhaps it is best to start with the individual, to consider whether the drinking behaviour is causing problems for either him or for other people and to decide whether you, as a professional, can do anything to help that person within the given confines of your professional role.

Whose problem?

This process of personal audit should also help to clarify whose the problem is. Is it a problem for the drinker, for a spouse or partner, for the family, for an employer, or for you, the professional worker? On occasion, professional workers may find themselves in the position of trying to do something positive about an alcohol or alcohol-related problem where the drinker has little or no inclination to do anything about it. This can be a very disabling experience as the worker takes on an increasing responsibility to achieve positive action and the drinker, conversely, accepts less and less responsibility for his behaviour and its outcomes. At this point it is worth clarifying not only whose the problem is, but also where the balance of control and power lies between the worker and the client or patient. If advice to a client or patient is to 'cut down consumption by three drinks per day', is it because the worker considers this to be the best solution, that the client considers it so, or have the worker and client discussed the issue and agreed, jointly, that this is the best solution? Professional workers should be wary of imposing their own values on a client's life style and of promoting courses of action or changes in behaviour that are not fully understood and agreed by the client or patient, as targets for change that have been imposed rarely succeed.

Chapter two

Deciding where we stand

Professional workers often feel uncomfortable about discussing a client's drinking behaviour and feel that they are trespassing in a private area that does not concern them. They tend to feel deskilled in the fact of an alcohol problem about which they have been given no specific training and are doubtful whether they have the right to intervene or whether they have the skills needed for intervention. On top of such uncertainty lies a nagging doubt about whether intervention on the part of the worker can achieve anything positive or whether it is simply better (and easier) to refer the client to an agency or organization that specializes in helping people with drinking problems. Much of this uncertainty arises from the way in which concepts of alcohol problems have developed since the turn of this century and the effects that predominant concepts have had on our attitudes and behaviour with regard to alcohol and alcohol-related problems.

Throughout Queen Victoria's reign there was an increasing demand for licensing legislation to regulate the hours during which alcohol could be sold. In the second half of the nineteenth century numerous temperance societies were formed, dedicated not only to saving people from the evil of alcohol, but also to providing better housing and educational and recreational opportunities (Williams and Brake 1980:4–11). The Temperance Movement quickly became a political issue and was hotly debated on all sides of the House. At the annual meeting of the United Kingdom Alliance in 1900, the President, Sir Wilfred Lawson, roused his audience by saying:

> There stands the liquor traffic and here stands the army, the Prohibition army, marshalled for the noblest work ever allotted to humanity. Turn aside, if you please, by the by-paths of

compromise and you are lost. Go straight and your ultimate triumph is as certain as the rising of tomorrow's sun.

(Lawson 1900:779)

It was a popular movement, partly because its supporters found it comfortable to range themselves on the side of good and morally condemn those deemed to be on the side of evil. As a concept of alcohol problems however, the 'good versus evil' idea did not go far enough and many began to question whether there were reasons — other than simply being bad — that might cause someone to get into difficulties with alcohol.

Alcoholics Anonymous, AA, a self-help group based on the disease concept, was founded in the USA and established in Britain in 1947. Although not seen by its members as a temperance society, AA aims to help those who attend the group meetings to achieve sobriety. Members consider their drinking problems as a disease and admit to themselves and others that they are powerless over alcohol. They follow the 'Twelve Steps of Alcoholics Anonymous' and share their drinking experience and recovery progress at regular group meetings.

In 1951, the World Health Organization set up an expert committee to consider the alcohol issue and to produce a definition of alcoholism. Not satisfied with its first definition, the committee met again the following year and put forward the notion that people who experienced problems with alcohol were ill and in need of treatment (Grant and Gwinner 1979:42–3). Although not a new idea, the notion of illness and treatment became known as the 'disease concept' and had far-ranging effects — still felt today — for both those in difficulties with alcohol and those trying to help. Temperance societies aimed to help people abandon drinking altogether and, by means of education about the nature and effects of alcohol, to persuade individuals to become abstainers. Close links with the churches ensured that the Movement had moral appeal. This was considered a great attraction by the Movement's supporters although the drinkers themselves were not as convinced. The problem of excessive drinking remained and another motivation had to be found to persuade people to abstain. Some drinkers found the disease concept an attractive one as it seemed to suggest that they were in no way responsible for their condition and had, rather, a respectable illness that required specialist treatment. Some professional workers also found it easy to accept the disease concept as it seemed to set the drinker in a more manageable context of a range of symptoms, an identifiable illness and subsequent recommendations for treatment. Treatment — usually seen as the responsibility of a specialist or a medic — was also viewed as a long-term process with little or no guarantee of a successful outcome. The alcohol field has gone on to develop many other concepts of alcohol problems — based on dependence or biological, psychological, or socio-cultural factors — but, although the disease concept has been largely discredited, its impact on thinking about alcohol problems remains.

This leaves us with a worker who may feel he has no right to intervene in a client's drinking, has few of the skills needed, is not a specialist and is uncertain about the positive outcome of any intervention he may propose. The client, on the other hand, may also feel that the worker has no right to intervene, that his drinking is not problematic and, even if it were, it would be the responsibility of someone else to treat him and make him better. It is worthwhile defining such feelings both for ourselves and our clients, and acknowledging that they will influence our attitudes and our approach to alcohol education. We should be aware of how our own process of socialization has influenced our attitudes to alcohol and shaped our drinking behaviour (see Chapter 1) and how the attitudes and behaviour of clients may have been similarly influenced and shaped. The worker must also acknowledge that his client may be physically and/or psychologically dependent on alcohol and may, genuinely, be unable to see that his drinking is causing problems. Having reached some common ground through discussion with the client, the professional worker should also assess the client's perceived ability to change behaviour that may, in turn, be affected by previous successes or failures.

Determining a rationale

Educating people about alcohol is different from educating them about philosophy or teaching them how to ride a bike. Alcohol education does involve increasing knowledge and developing skills, but should never neglect to explore attitudes, feelings, and values. It is as important for the worker to do this himself as it is to do it with a client or patient. Workers might find it helpful to do some of the exercises from Chapter 7 and 8 themselves, before attempting to do them with a client. The exercises are designed not only to increase knowledge about alcohol but also to allow individuals to explore their attitudes to drinking.

Many people are dubious about the effectiveness of alcohol educa-tion and, by simply seeing it as a process of imparting factual informa-tion, judge alcohol education to have failed if the information is not acted upon. Such people should ask themselves whether they are in the business of wishing to control their clients' behaviour or whether they wish to empower them to make informed decisions about their own behaviour. The issue of control is a crucial one in alcohol education and, again, it must be emphasized that all work should begin with the client and progress outwards rather than the professional workers arriving with a predetermined programme of education that they intend to impose on the clients.

To facilitate this process and to develop a personal rationale for alcohol education, professionals may find it helpful to begin by considering what they can offer to the client or patient. Although many workers feel inadequate when dealing with the topic of alcohol, the skills needed for alcohol education are the same as those developed during the basic training of most professionals. These include the ability to listen, advise, support, assess, and evaluate and may require personal qualities of empathy, patience, and enthusiasm. A sound factual basis for education is necessary and workers may need to improve or update their knowledge in this respect (see the recommended reading). It is also important to clarify what you expect your alcohol education to achieve and to plan it accordingly. This aspect will be covered in more detail in Chapters 5 and 6.

Finally, almost every professional worker will have experience or knowledge of a client or patient with an alcohol problem who seems to have had contact with every alcohol agency imaginable and who, despite various forms of help and intervention, has done nothing to modify his drinking. In such cases, it is easy to say that, as nothing appears to work for that individual, any further attempts to intervene on the worker's part are invalid and pointless. There are, indeed, some drinkers who seem determined to damage themselves in this way but, as discussed in Chapter 1, they rarely exist in total isolation. The worker should ask himself whether intervention in the form of alcohol education may be helpful to the spouse, to family members, or to relatives even though it may not appear to be immediately helpful to the drinker. Alcohol education can play a major role in helping families affected by an individual's drinking by exploring alternative coping strategies, increasing self-esteem and self-control, and by helping them both to identify and avoid game-playing situations. Professionals may find it useful to work through the practical exercises given at the end of this chapter to help them clarify and improve their role as an alcohol educator.

What is alcohol education?

Alcohol education, along with many other strategies for drug education, is often put under the broad heading of prevention and yet what we are trying to prevent remains unclarified and nebulous. In the case of alcohol, are we trying to prevent people drinking altogether, or to prevent them drinking in a harmful way, or are our efforts to be aimed at high-risk groups such as young people or pregnant women to prevent them damaging themselves? McKechnie puts forward three meanings for the term prevention:

1. stopping, or to keep from coming to pass
2. hindering, to make it difficult for something to come about, to take place or happen
3. curtailing, or holding steady the frequency of occurrences at their present level, preventing them increasing.

(McKechnie 1985:197–213)

Applied to alcohol problems, this means that education could aim to stop alcohol problems ever arising, or to make it difficult for alcohol problems to arise or to prevent any increase in the number of alcohol problems from the present level. Depending on the particular aim chosen, objectives might include banning alcohol, reducing per capita consumption, or enabling people to avoid or free themselves from dependence on alcohol.

Traditionally, prevention is divided into three types — primary, secondary, and tertiary — based on the concept of prevention used in community medicine. In the case of alcohol:

1. Primary prevention would be aimed at healthy people — would-be or moderate drinkers — and would seek to educate them about alcohol to enable them to enjoy it and avoid any harmful effects.
2. Secondary prevention would be aimed at those who may be in the early stages of developing an alcohol problem and would seek to identify problems at the earliest possible stage and prevent them becoming chronic or irreversible. It would also be aimed at special groups within the population thought to be particularly vulnerable to alcohol problems or in need of alcohol education.
3. Tertiary prevention would be aimed at those known to be damaging themselves by their drinking and would seek to encourage them to

accept treatment and to maximize their remaining potential for healthy living.

Any professional intending to use alcohol education in the course of a working relationship with a client or patient would find it helpful to clarify which stage the client is at and to formulate the aims and objectives of the education accordingly (see Table 2.1).

Table 2.1 Aims and objectives of three levels of prevention

	Aims	*Objectives*
Primary	To educate about alcohol and its effects	To increase factual knowledge about alcohol
		To explore attitudes to alcohol
Secondary	To promote early identification of problems	To increase knowledge of safe/harmful levels of drinking.
	To prevent problems becoming chronic or irreversible	To encourage awareness of types of help available
Tertiary	To encourage client to accept treatment	To increase self-esteem
	To maximize remaining potential for healthy enjoyable life	To increase potential for self-management
		To explore alternative coping strategies

It is advisable to attempt something on a small scale which, if well thought-out and properly planned, stands a good chance of success, rather than a large-scale, sweeping intervention without clearly defined aims and objectives. It is easy for the worker to offer general advice about 'cutting down' and 'drinking sensibly', but, unless the pros and cons of doing so are fully explored and firm guidelines given and skills practised to achieve this, the advice is likely to be meaningless to the drinker.

Over the last ten years, increasing recognition has been given to the potential of many health and welfare professionals to become involved and play a role in alcohol education. They undoubtedly have the skills to implement alcohol education and often have more frequent and appropriate opportunities to do so than the specialists on whose 'territory' they imagine they encroach. Those whose work is based in the community such as health visitors, community psychiatric nurses, and midwives, often have the opportunity to see clients and patients in their own homes and to talk to them in a relaxed setting, more conducive to frank discussion than an office or surgery. Others such as probation officers, social workers, and youth and community workers, are able to build a long-term, working relationship with some clients and establish the trust and rapport needed to explore personal or emotive issues. Such unique advantages are often underestimated by professionals and yet, in a study of people with alcohol problems who attended an education and awareness programme at an alcohol treatment unit in Canterbury, 'every indication is given that experiences associated with trust, dependability, understanding and acceptance and encouragement were considered to be the most "helpful" therapeutic experiences' (Cartwright 1985:124–6). When asked to consider the truth of various statements and rank them in order of helpfulness, at least 85 per cent of those taking part in the study highlighted the importance of such aspects to them personally (see Table 2.2).

Table 2.2 Is treatment an effective way of helping clients?

Items considered true by at least 85% of the sample and ranked in order of their helpfulness

Felt there was a member of staff whom I could depend upon and trust

Felt there was at least one member of staff who understood and accepted me

Felt there was at least one person who understood and accepted me

Felt there was someone whom I could depend upon and trust

Received suggestions and advice from staff about the things I could do in the future

Learnt a lot of facts related to my difficulties

Been able to see my life from a different perspective

Felt understood by another person

Learnt that I am not the only person with my type of problem

Been able to view myself and others in a new light

Been able to get things off my chest

Received definite suggestions about the ways to handle my problems

Been encouraged by the knowledge that others had been helped

Been encouraged by improvements in other people

Learnt that I must take ultimate responsibility for my new life no matter how much guidance and support I get from others

Revealed embarrassing things about myself and yet still felt accepted

Belonged to a group of people who understood and accepted me

Source: Cartwright, A. (1985).

It would be a mistake to ignore such information or to underestimate the value clients and patients may place on developing trust and rapport with the worker, receiving advice and guidance and being given an opportunity for self-expression. Obviously, some of the statements rated highly by the sample refer to benefits they received from taking part in group sessions and this may not be an option that every worker can offer. Much will depend on the type and range of services available in each area. Details of how to identify what is available are given in Chapter 10.

Clarifying and improving your role

By this stage readers are, hopefully, feeling more positive about alcohol education in general and are willing to consider clarifying and improving their own role. The following practical exercises were originally designed 'to help health professionals to recognise the health education elements which are integrated into all kinds of every day work' (Ewles and Simnett 1985:52). They have been amended to allow readers to focus on their educational style and philosophy and on how they feel about being an alcohol educator (exercise 2.1), to clarify their role as an alcohol educator (exercise 2.2), and to improve that role and identify what helps and hinders work in alcohol education (exercise 2.3).

Exercise 2.1: You as an alcohol educator

Purpose The purpose of this exercise is to help you to focus on your educational philosophy and style and how you feel about yourself as an educator.

Preparation You can do this exercise alone, but it is better to do it with a partner, taking it in turns to be speaker and listener.

Method The job of the speaker is to think and speak and, at the end of each section, to summarize his conclusions; the job of the listener is to listen, to ask a question if the speaker gets stuck, and to help the speaker to summarize at the end, if he should ask for help.

1. *Your alcohol-education philosophy.*

   Describe your alcohol education philosophy. Some questions you could ask yourself are:

What do I think my alcohol education is for?
What is the ideal relationship between me as an educator and my client as a learner?
Do I regard myself primarily as a facilitator (helping people to help themselves) or as a teacher (who provides answers)?

2. *Your strengths and weaknesses as an alcohol educator.*

   List and describe your strengths and weaknesses. Try to keep a balance between positive and negative. Do this for all kinds of educational methods — counselling, group work, one-to-one work, teaching, instructing, advising.

3. *How you feel about yourself as an alcohol educator?*

   Try to put into words your feelings about yourself as an alcohol educator. Some questions you could ask yourself are:

   How do I feel about myself when I am educating clients?
   What kind of educator am I?
   Do I have one standard for myself and another for clients?

4. *How do you want to change?*

   Some questions you could ask yourself are:

   Do I want to rethink my attitudes towards clients?
   Do I want to learn to use new communication styles?
   Do I want to develop my skills in different educational methods?

Exercise 2.2: Clarifying your role as an alcohol educator

Purpose The following is a list of types of activity you may undertake as part of your job that may have an educational element. (We have excluded many other types of activity — such as administration — which do not have an educational element.)

Teaching clients	Working with groups
Caring	Structuring therapy
Treating clients	Counselling
Supporting	Advising
Inspecting	Assessing

25

Planning	Evaluating
Referring	Working with colleagues
Teaching students/colleagues	

Method

1. Add any other activities with an alcohol education element that are important in your job.
2. Tick the activities you undertake.
3. Identify the educational aspects of each of these activities, giving examples.

Exercise 2.3: What helps and hinders your alcohol education work?

Purpose This is a force-field analysis exercise. It is designed to help you to identify helping and hindering forces in your own situation.

Method In a stable system, the forces for producing changes are equally offset by forces opposed to change. It is essential to pinpoint all the possible helping and hindering forces, so that you can take steps to increase the power of helping forces. This disruption of the balance of forces results in progress towards change. For your own situation:

— make a list of forces that help you and forces that hinder you, in your alcohol-education work;

— identify ways of increasing the helping forces and ways of decreasing the hindering forces.

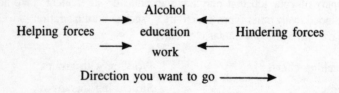

26

Chapter three

Identifying the influences at work

Earlier chapters have considered some of the many influences at work
that shape our attitudes to alcohol but it is also worthwhile concentrating
on the factors that influence our decisions and subsequent behaviour. Why
is it that we are more likely to have several drinks in a cosy pub in the
company of friends or at an office party than we are at a church social
where punch is the only beverage on offer? Factors that influence our decision to drink alcohol are numerous and complex and have resulted in a
number of models being put forward to explain this behaviour. One such
model, developed by Tones (1987:305-17), shows the major psychological
and social influences on health behaviour (see Figure 3.1). There are three
systems — normative, belief, and motivational — that influence our decision to drink alcohol or not and regulate how much and how frequently
we drink. In addition, there are a number of facilitating and inhibiting
factors that determine whether our intention to behave in a certain way
is actually translated into behaviour. Tones explains that:

> attempts to explain or predict behaviour or devise an educational
> programme will be more successful if highly specific health
> actions are identified, for instance an offer from a specific
> person such as a friend. This principle is similar to that proposed
> by Fishbein (Fishbein and Ajzen, 1975, Ajzen and Fishbein,
> 1980) to whom HAM is indebted for certain of its definitions _
> and theoretical formulations. Secondly, the importance of
> feedback should be noted. Once an individual has made a
> decision, the effect of that decision will make itself felt, either in
> the short or longer term, by affecting either the Belief System or
> the Motivation System or both.

(Tones 1987:308-9)

Figure 3.1 The health-action model: an overview

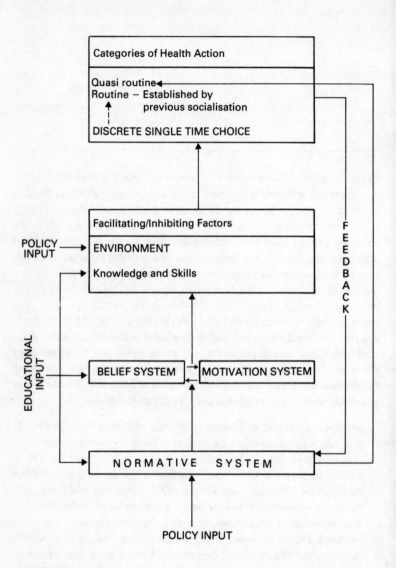

Source: Tones, B.K. (1987).

The normative system

Social norms and expectations play a large part in influencing our behaviour whatever the context in which we find ourselves drinking. Norms are conventional ways of doing things, accepted by the majority and indicated by areas of behaviour where sanctions, rules, or laws apply. For instance, it is a social norm to drink alcohol at 'New Year' or at a party but not to do so first thing in the morning or while driving a car. Norms are always evolving as society reviews what constitutes acceptable or unacceptable behaviour and 'they may vary in different localities and situations, according to the social groups to which a person belongs, but in each case, failure to conform to norms may lead to ostracism' (Howe and Wright 1987;112–13). In the case of alcohol, if all your friends are heavy drinkers and you prefer not to drink, you may run the risk of being rejected by your friends because you do not conform to their 'group' norms. Similarly, in a family context where drinking alcohol is acceptable — and possibly expected on special occasions — a teetotal relative might arouse curiosity, be teased or even termed a 'spoilsport' because he does not conform to family norms. There are many different types of group norms — family, friends, colleagues — that can affect a drinker's behaviour and it may be helpful for workers to encourage their clients to clarify them for themselves and to be aware of the benefits and drawbacks involved in conforming or failing to conform.

The belief system

Beliefs 'deal with a person's understanding of himself and his environment' (Fishbein and Ajzen 1975:131) and are based on personal experience, direct observation, or information received from other sources. Beliefs form an information base that allows an individual to develop attitudes and intentions to behave in a certain way. Beliefs play an important part in determining behaviour and there are several examples of alcohol-related beliefs that will affect a drinker's behaviour:

1 *Cause-and-effect beliefs.* 'If one drink makes me feel this good, two drinks will make me feel twice as good!'
2 *Belief in the seriousness of the consequences.* 'It's only the hard spirit drinkers who cause themselves harm. Beer drinkers are safe.'
3 *Belief in the effectiveness of a course of action.* 'Cutting down to

three drinks a day won't really make much difference to my stomach ulcer.'

4 *Belief in the 'costs' of a course of action.* 'Cutting down to three drinks a day will be so difficult, I would rather carry on as I am now and put up with my stomach ulcer.'

Workers will find it helpful to clarify what clients believe about their drinking and its consequences and should not be surprised if the beliefs expressed are at variance with the way in which workers perceive reality. Some people prefer to believe myths about alcohol or to accept things that are patently untrue if this allows them to continue their drinking behaviour undisturbed. The latter part of this chapter will examine some of the more common myths and misunderstandings in an attempt to understand how they arise and why they endure.

The motivational system

In the motivational system, a person's attitudes, values, and drives are important. Attitudes are ways of thinking, feeling, believing about, or reacting to a subject and are acquired during the process of socialization. They affect the way in which a person reacts to a subject or situation and, in the case of alcohol, will influence whether that person drinks or not, how often he drinks and the extent to which he drinks. A man who holds the attitude that drunkenness is part of having a good time, is unlikely to stop after two beers if he is enjoying himself! Conversely, if a woman holds the attitude that tipsiness is one of the first signs of moral collapse, she is unlikely to drink more than moderately, even in a heavy-drinking context.

Values are what an individual considers to be important and, in the case of drinking, might include valuing relaxation, the drug effect, the role of being a heavy drinker, or the conviviality of the public house. Such positive payoffs derived from drinking alcohol fulfill needs that we all have but may satisfy in other ways. Maslow (1943) states that an individual's needs are organized in a hierarchical fashion (see Figure 3.2) so that basic drives for food, shelter, and reproduction need to be met before other less basic drives — for love, popularity, self-esteem — are considered. It has been suggested that physical and/or psychological dependence on alcohol may have a similar status to basic needs in that they can override socially acquired values and attitudes and exert a powerful influence on behaviour.

Figure 3.2 Maslow's hierarchy of human needs

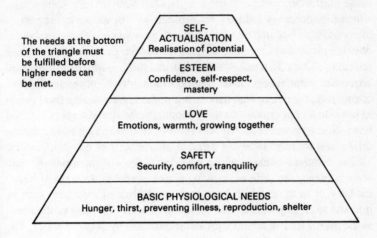

The needs at the bottom of the triangle must be fulfilled before higher needs can be met.

SELF-ACTUALISATION
Realisation of potential

ESTEEM
Confidence, self-respect, mastery

LOVE
Emotions, warmth, growing together

SAFETY
Security, comfort, tranquility

BASIC PHYSIOLOGICAL NEEDS
Hunger, thirst, preventing illness, reproduction, shelter

Source: Maslow, A.H. (1943).

The combined effects of these three systems — normative, belief, motivational — will result in an individual intending to act in a certain way but that intention, in turn, may also be affected by certain conditions or circumstances that will influence whether or not the intention is translated into behaviour. A man trying to cut down his alcohol consumption may intend to go home to watch television. His actual behaviour, however, may be affected by whether he meets a crowd of friends in the pub who urge him to stay, whether he only has enough money for two pints, or whether he can afford more and how interested he is in the television programmes! Throughout this whole process, the drug effect of alcohol will also influence his mood and decision-making abilities.

The importance of context

The context in which we drink is also important as differing contexts will have differing effects on our drinking behaviour. Historical precedent may have influenced — and continue to influence — the drinking patterns of society but, at a more local level, it may also dictate the pattern and range of drinking places available in the community. Geographic areas, which rely on heavy industry for prosperity — or did so in the past — often have an accompanying legacy of an above-average number of drinking places and a population with a raised level of alcohol and alcohol-related problems. In areas — both urban and rural — which have suffered economic deprivation and fragmentation of a once tightly-knit community, the pub or club may be one of the few remaining focal points to provide an opportunity to meet people, make friends, socialize, and relax. Social norms in such places revolve around buying and accepting drinks and those who do not drink at all are seen as non-conformers.

The cultural context in which we drink is equally important and may even influence the style of drinking places available. In areas of heavy industry or in those which have seen the decline of industries such as iron and steel, shipbuilding and coal-mining, heavy drinking is often seen as the prerogative of adult males and is emulated by younger males. The prevalence of heavy drinking and its acceptance as the norm is sometimes reflected in the style of pubs or clubs available, which are frequently bereft of comfortable furnishings and do not offer alternative facilities for food or entertainment. Women are rarely welcome in such places as heavy drinking is associated with being macho or manly and it is feared women might detract from or interfere with the business of consumption. Double standards with regard to men's and women's drinking exist in many countries and often reflect women's perceived place in society. Drinking behaviour that is acceptable, condoned, and approved of in a man may be unacceptable, disapproved, or denigrated in a woman. There are many reasons for the existence of such double standards — political, cultural, socio-economic — not least of which is the perceived prime role of women to nurture or care for others, which might be severely impaired by excessive alcohol consumption. With the progress of emancipation however, standards relating to patterns of some women's drinking are beginning to change and breweries have quickly modified the style of some of their establishments to attract the new clientele. Alcohol consumption is increasing among women drinkers and 'levels of alcohol misuse among women have risen in association with the upsurge in alcohol consumption that occurred during the 1960's and 1970's' (Royal College of Psychiatrists 1986: 71-2.) Consumption has risen among young women in particular as wine bars and cocktail bars provide an attractive, sophisticated environment in which to socialize with friends and, particularly, to meet members of the opposite sex. Other cultural developments include the greater emphasis placed on leisure and recreation time and the ever-increasing number of sports clubs and leisure centres. As discussed in Chapter 2, alcohol helps to smoothe the transition between 'work' and 'leisure' time and it is rare to see a new snooker and pool hall or leisure centre being built without the added facility of a bar. There is nothing intrinsically problematic about this but drinking, once seen as an adjunct to leisure and recreation, has almost become an integral part of such activities and, in an age of increasing, widescale unemployment, we should be concerned for those who have nothing but leisure time to fill.

The influence of the media

Today, most people regularly watch television, read a daily newspaper, or take a weekly magazine and are subject to the media's portrayal of alcohol in society. Those working in the media argue that they simply reflect reality and do not glamorize or aggrandize the place or role of alcohol, although some accept a certain degree of social responsibility and are ready to consider closely the messages they promote. In his paper on 'The Portrayal of alcohol on television', Anders Hansen proposes that 'television provides a steady continuous flow of images of alcohol and drinking, it provides a pool of readily available values, norms, information and frameworks of understanding through which social reality may be interpreted' (Hansen 1986). Most commonly on television, alcohol is associated with relaxation and enjoyment, smooth social functioning, success, or sophistication. The type of alcohol consumed — wine, spirits, cocktails, champagne — may be used to convey information about an individual's status or social success or may be used to indicate hospitality and largesse. Hansen notes that 'it seems that television reflects and gives currency to beliefs that wine drinking is associated with glamorous and affluent lifestyles, while beer drinking has a masculine and downmarket quality to it.' The more serious side of drinking alcohol or excessive drinking is not as frequently portrayed and it is less common to see alcohol associated with accidents, fights or relationship problems. 'The relative absence of any portrayal of negative or problematic outcomes of alcohol consumption contrasts with the frequent occurrence of alcohol consumption, where a character is often shown drinking on several separate occasions in the course of a programme' (Hansen, 1986). Even hangovers become risible as those suffering are laughed at or ridiculed. The more serious consequences of drinking are thus minimized, if they are represented at all. A standard setting for many soap operas is the bar or lounge of the public house — a neat contrivance that enables script writers to assemble large numbers of characters at once, gives them an opportunity for brief interchanges and allows them to depart once their lines have been spoken. The frequent consumption of alcohol in such settings tends to suggest that drinking alcohol is a normal, acceptable way of life with few or no detrimental consequences. Alcohol advertising perpetuates this theme as it urges people to drink one brew or another suggesting that it is all that is needed to become one of the crowd, to have a good time, or — in the case of women — to appear sexy, mysterious, or sophisticated. The actual taste of the beverage is rarely emphasized, but rather the setting and its perceived attributes and effects. In the United Kingdom in 1975 the Advertising Standards Authority drew up a code of practice relating to the advertising of alcoholic drinks and stated that:

> the Alcoholic Drinks industry, with others, is aware that a small but significant minority cause harm to themselves and others through misuse of alcohol. They share the concern about this social problem, the causes of which are complex and varied. There is no evidence connecting such misuse with the advertising of alcoholic drinks.
>
> (Williams and Brake 1980: 599–601)

Since then, further restrictions on the advertising of alcoholic drinks have been imposed and, although there is no direct evidence to suggest a causal link between alcohol advertising and alcohol misuse, the influential power of the media should not be underestimated.

What about the drinker?

Aside from the historical, social, cultural, and media influences, what happens to the drinker when he takes a drink? In Chapter 1 we have seen that for many people their first taste of alcohol is a disappointment but that, partly due to some of the aforementioned influences, many people continue to use alcohol until they learn to appreciate and enjoy its effects. Throughout this learning process, alcohol becomes synonymous with fun, relaxation, companionship, reward, and celebration although a particularly bad hangover or extended binge might alter that view temporarily or even permanently. Many young people cite the time they got drunk on cider, perhaps, or rum and state that they have never touched it since and only have to smell it to remember how ill and nauseous they felt. They carry on drinking other types of alcoholic drink, nevertheless, because their investment in and enjoyment of drinking is stronger and more treasured than the memory of the hangover or illness. For other people, however, only one experience of intoxication or illness through excessive consumption is enough to persuade them never to drink alcohol again. This is most likely to be the case among women drinkers, who possibly have a weaker investment in drinking and, because of societal norms, are less likely to suffer censure or ostracism if they do not drink at all.

A further bonus to drinking alcohol is its drug effect (ethanol) or the attraction of instant pleasure and reward. If alcohol did not have such an effect, it is unlikely that many people would drink it or that multinational corporations would be able to make vast amounts of money from its production and sale. There are many other ways to relax, to celebrate, to wind down, or to have fun but, apart from other drug substances, they tend not to have the bonus or the immediate reward of alcohol. Depending on the amount of food present in the drinker's stomach, alcohol passes quickly from the stomach and small intestine into the bloodstream and is carried rapidly throughout the body affecting, among others, the most sensitive organ, the brain. Once in the brain, alcohol firstly affects the centres that control inhibitions, judgements, and reasoning and this often gives rise to the myth that alcohol is a stimulant as drinkers experience the release of inhibition and tend to talk more loudly and crack more jokes. Discrimination, memory, concentration, and insight become dulled and, if drinking continues, gradually submerged. For many people, this is an attractive quality of alcohol for they are not necessarily drunk but are able to enjoy the depressant effects of alcohol as it slows them down and gradually releases their inhibitions while appearing, paradoxically, to pep them up and stimulate them. Further drinking will affect the drinker's motor processes so that he finds it increasingly difficult to co-ordinate body movements and may be prone to quick changes in mood and sudden emotional outbursts. Some drinkers put this to good effect and allow their drinking to trigger angry, emotional, or violent outbursts that would not normally be expressed during sobriety. The part of the brain controlling the senses is also gradually affected as the drinker's field of vision narrows, sounds become distorted, and hearing levels lowered. Eventually the senses of smell, taste, and touch will also be impaired and, if more alcohol is consumed, the processes of respiration may be affected and breathing may eventually cease. Obviously most people stop drinking, are ill, or pass out before this stage is reached or are content to moderate their drinking so that they experience the earlier drug effects of alcohol. Although the latter drug effects — changes in mood and impairment of senses — might not seem desirable to most people, they may be considered attractive by a minority who want the short-term respite or oblivion they offer (see Chapter 7, Table 7.5).

The drinker's family

Just as the drinker's behaviour will have an effect on the members of his family, so the family will influence the way in which the drinker behaves. It is easy for families to become hooked into the 'game' or 'games' played by the drinker and to find it difficult to alter the dynamics by which they function. The 'games' theory of transactional analysis is one way of considering and assessing interactions within families. It is important for professional workers to be aware of the existence of such 'games', to increase their clients' and families' awareness of them and, above all, to avoid being drawn into them themselves! In *Games Alcoholics Play*, Claude Steiner defines a 'game' as 'a behaviour sequence which 1) is an orderly series of transactions with a beginning and an end; 2) contains an ulterior motive, that is, a psychological level different from the social level; and 3) results in a payoff for both players' (Steiner 1971:11.) In the case of a family affected by an individual's drinking a 'game' might involve a series of transactions or conversational exchanges where the ulterior motive is never explicit and where alcohol is used as a trigger for avoidance of problems — emotional, sexual, financial — for violence, attention–seeking behaviour, or physical exit from the scene. A typical 'game' might be:

Husband. I'm going out to see the football match down at the park.
Wife. Well I hope you are not going to go to the pub on the way back.
Husband. If I do, it will only be for a couple of beers.
Wife. You had better not come home drunk this time!
Husband. I'll come home how I like; that is if I come home at all!
Wife. That's typical of you going out leaving me on my own,

just when I have cooked a nice meal for us both.

Husband. Don't start nagging at me again. That's your trouble — look I've got to go.

The husband wants to go out for a drink and the wife does not want him to but neither states the case clearly. The wife makes threats about him returning home drunk and he responds by threatening not to come home at all. Neither is being clear about what they want or do not want; both are using the drinking as a bone of contention. The wife gets a little nearer the truth with her final statement ('you don't appreciate me'), which the husband chooses to interpret as nagging thus giving him the excuse he needs to absent himself from the scene.

Steiner (1971) goes on to describe an individual's life as a chain of games, each game leading to a preconceived goal and develops the idea of games particularly played by drinkers which was first put forward by his associate Eric Berne in his book *Games People Play*. Steiner develops three particular games worthy of consideration, not only for the frequency with which they are played in drinkers' families, but also for the potential they have to draw the unwary professional worker into the game.

1. *'Drunk and Proud'*. The drinker puts himself in the position of being disapproved of and uses drinking as a means of indulging in other forms of misbehaviour such as anger or violence. When intoxicated, the drinker will appear uncaring about the consequences of his behaviour and when sober, will blame the misbehaviour on the effects of alcohol. While the game is allowed to continue, the drinker is not particularly interested in being helped as he gets his reward in the form of attention from the spouse/partner. The drinker is often rebelling against persecuting parents or a domineering, possessive spouse. The spouse appears blameless — although is usually not — and allows the game to continue by alternating between the role of persecutor or victim. The professional worker should be wary of being coerced into playing one or either of these roles and should encourage both drinker and spouse to develop assertiveness skills and accept family or group therapy.

2. *'Lush'* or *'Nobody loves me'*. This game is often played in response to emotional and/or sexual deprivation and involves the drinker using alcohol to cover up the inadequacies of a particular relationship. Often played with a partner who is unable to offer emotional and/or sexual

fulfillment, the game ensures that such inadequacies are never brought into the open, admitted, or confronted. The worker should encourage both partners to accept joint therapy and should help them consider how they can both offer a greater degree of emotional and/or sexual fulfillment. If this does not succeed or if one or both partners refuse to cooperate, it may be necessary to consider ending the relationship.

3. *'Wino' or 'I'm sick to death'*. This is a self-destructive game in which the drinker gains attention by making himself ill through excessive and/or long-term consumption. Due to the long-term effects of alcohol, both physical and psychological, it may not be possible to reverse the game. The drinker forces other people to take care of him — treatment agencies, the police, the courts — and the worker, caught up in the game, might be left feeling that the outlook is bleak and that practical intervention such as vitamin injections, lifts to the courts or unemployment offices, or help with state benefits are the only things left to offer. Unfortunately such 'help' allows the drinker to take less and less responsibility for himself and to expect an increasing amount of support from the worker. Steiner 1971 puts forward a more optimistic outlook, however, and states:

> the evidence shows that even the most severe 'Wino' player is
> capable of stopping his self-destruction; the annals of AA are full
> of examples. Those who apply the theories of transactional
> analysis to alcohol problems tend to feel that since alcoholism is
> a game, a person can choose not to play. Because they believe
> the alcoholic can affect his own life situation, they tend to avoid
> expressions of pity, empathy, or even compassion, and insist that
> the alcoholic take responsbility for his behaviour.

(Steiner 1971:82)

There are many things the professional worker can do to prevent the continuation of such 'games'. Workers can encourage clients and their families to be aware of 'game playing' and to explore alternative, more open ways of communicating and achieving the payoff sought. They can also avoid being drawn into the 'game' themselves, whether as victim, persecutor, or rescuer (see Chapter 8, Figure 8.2) and should be ready to give unexpected responses and reactions to roles so as to challenge players, encourage them to accept responsibility for their behaviour, and prevent the continuation of the 'game'. As there are no true winners in these 'games' and each payoff is won at some cost or sacrifice, it is helpful to encourage players to work towards compromise or 'to look for a solution, or negotiate a contract that does not result in either party losing face, or being put down' (Simmett, Wright, and Evans 1983:69).

Intervention may not always be readily welcomed, however, as the 'games' often take the place of honest, open communication and allow the players to avoid confronting deep-seated or painful problems. As stated earlier, each game also involves payoffs for its players who may resent their particular payoff being threatened or removed altogether and may feel unsettled when their given roles are challenged or changed. Such challenges must be made, however, if progress is to be made and a more honest form of communication is to be developed.

Myths and misunderstandings about alcohol

For all the true qualities possessed by alcohol — some of which we have already considered — there are as many, if not more, perceived or imagined qualities that people equally hold to be true. There are many reasons for such myths and misunderstandings due partly to the role alcohol has played throughout history, its use in religious ceremonies and its ability to alter our level of consciousness. Several myths endure because they are, in part, based on fact, or more accurately, on an imperfect understanding of fact. Also, as stated earlier, people tend to accept or reject factual information according to how it accords with their belief system and whether acceptance of the information requires any major changes in behaviour.

Some myths and misunderstandings about alcohol are so common that they are worth enumerating here in an attempt to see how they arise and why they endure.

1. *Alcohol is a stimulant.* Alcohol affects the centres in the brain that control inhibitions, reasoning, and judgement. As the drinker experiences a gradual lessening of constraint on inhibition, he may feel not only light-headed but also light-hearted. The early stages of a party or celebration are often accompanied by people laughing loudly, talking freely, and appearing unusually stimulated. This is often mistakenly attributed to the so-called stimulant effect of alcohol.

2. *Alcohol helps you to sleep.* If you drink enough alcohol, it will certainly knock you out and put you to sleep very quickly. Alcohol, however, interferes with sleep patterns and does not promote restful,

refreshing sleep. A small nightcap may help you to relax sufficiently to sleep but you should be wary if the nightcap gets larger and larger or appears to have a diminishing effect.

3. *Alcohol keeps you warm.* This is an enduring myth promoted in part, by the apparent burning or warming effect induced by drinking spirits — hence the St Bernard dogs carrying small barrels of brandy with which to revive travellers who have lost their way. In reality, alcohol has the opposite effect and speeds up heat loss by causing blood vessels near the surface of the skin to expand. As more blood flows near the surface of the skin, more body heat is lost. Large amounts of alcohol depress the hypothalamus, the mechanism controlling body temperature and may facilitate hypothermia (subnormal body temperature).

4. *Alcohol makes you sexy.* Alcohol, through its action on inhibitions, may induce you to act in a sexier way or, by affecting the processes of judgement, may encourage you to view the opposite sex as more attractive than usual! As Shakespeare said, alcohol 'provokes the desire, but takes away the performance'. Heavy drinking, in this way, contributes to the cause of sexual problems. However it may also ensue as a result of them.

5. *Alcohol acts as a food.* In Chapter 1, the concept of a 'liquid lunch' was highlighted. Many people consider alcohol to be a food substitute, imagining it to contain essential nutritional elements. Alcohol, in fact, contains mainly carbohydrates and, as such, does not represent a nutritionally balanced foodstuff (see Chapter 7, Table 7.4). Excessive alcohol consumption may also impair the body's ability to absorb vitamins and minerals and may lead to varying degrees of malnutrition.

6. *Spirit drinking is more harmful than beer drinking.* This myth arises from a simple misunderstanding about the facts relating to the strengths of different alcoholic drinks and is probably promoted most often by beer drinkers! The exercise on units of alcohol in Chapter 7, p. 97–9 shows that there is as much alcohol in a single measure of whisky as there is in a half pint of ordinary beer or lager. The drinker who has consumed five pints of beer has consumed the alcohol equivalent of ten single whiskies. In terms of alcohol-related damage, it is the amount of alcohol consumed and the frequency of consumption that is important rather than the type of alcoholic drink chosen.

7. *Drinking alcohol makes a man of you.* Drinking alcohol is often, mistakenly, associated with being manly, sporty, or virile. Younger males in particular tend to see heavy drinking as indicative of having reached manhood and nights spent in the company of like-minded friends are as much about consuming large quantities of alcohol as they are about enjoyment and relaxation. Some alcoholic drinks are reputed 'to sort the men from the boys', 'to make a man out of you', or even 'to put hairs on your chest' while, in reality, there is little that is manly or virile about drunkenness, severe hangovers, or beer guts! There is also a lack of understanding about the process of developing tolerance, which takes place as people increase their consumption. Alcohol also impairs physical fitness so sportsmen and sportswomen should take care to drink in moderation.

8. *Alcohol gives you confidence.* In small quantities, alcohol may help you to relax sufficiently to socialize more easily or to make a speech at a wedding but it can be detrimental on other occasions when a clear head is needed, such as at a job interview or when driving a car. Alcohol may also affect you paradoxically by making you *feel* you are acting in a more competent, confident manner, when in reality you are not.

9 *Hangover cures.* The number of cures purporting to alleviate the unpleasant effects of alcohol is legend but, unfortunately, few of them work. Some are devoted to rendering the drinker sober while others attempt to relieve the nausea, headaches, and diarrhoea that may accompany a hangover. Black coffee, cold showers, fresh air, and exercise will do little to sober the drinker, although he may feel more awake and alert. Such measures have no effect on the level of alcohol in the blood that governs the degree of intoxication. Time is the only factor that will lower the level of alcohol concentration in the blood (see Chapter 7, p. 102–4).

The congeners or impurities in some types of alcoholic drinks are more likely to induce hangovers than others (see Figure 3.3) and should, therefore, be consumed in moderation. Proprietary medicines designed to relieve the unpleasant effects of hangovers may help the sufferer who should also rest, drink plenty of fluids, and try to eat small meals regularly so as not to place undue strain on the digestive system, which may already be upset and irritated.

Finally the practice of taking 'a hair of the dog that bit you' — taking

Figure 3.3 Hangovers

Hangovers are caused by alcohol. And the best way to avoid a hangover is to drink less alcohol.

Dehydration is one of the problems. The alcohol in your drink tends to make the water move out of the body cells and accumulate in the blood.

Most alcoholic drinks also contain additives which give drinks their characteristic colour, flavour, smell and taste. These add to your hangover too. Some drinks contain more additives than others. Vodka has very few additives, while red wine, port and brandy have many.

But different drinks affect people in different ways so the only real way of avoiding a hangover is by being careful about how much you drink.

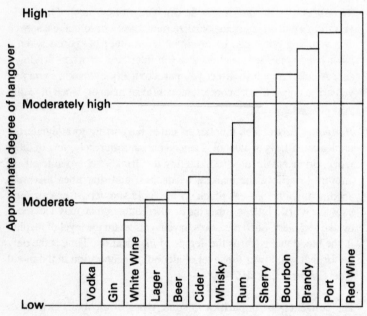

Approximate amount of additives in various unmixed drinks

Source: Health Education Council, 1986.

42

another alcoholic drink — should be avoided as it will not only merely stave off the side-effects of excessive consumption but may also lead to physical and/or psychological dependence on alcohol or relief drinking.

During the course of a working relationship with a client or patient, the worker should make every effort to understand the position of the client, the problem he perceives he has, and the influences at work on his drinking behaviour before attempting to implement alcohol education as part of an intervention strategy. It is also important to encourage the drinker to gain an understanding of such factors and to appreciate how they may shape his attitudes and influence his behaviour. Discussion of some of the common myths and misunderstandings about alcohol may prove a helpful starting point.

Chapter four

The place and role of alcohol education

In the alcohol field, there are many different types of intervention which are often grouped loosely under the umbrella term of 'treatment'. The sheer variety of terms — therapy, counselling, crisis intervention, relapse, prevention, and client education — used to describe different types of intervention with different aims and objectives, may leave the professional feeling confused and bewildered. There seems to be so much that is new and requires background reading and careful consideration before it can be assimilated into the workload, it is easy to understand why professionals might feel inadequate or deskilled and might prefer to fall back on the comforting thought that dealing with alcohol problems is, after all, a job for the specialist worker. To do so, however, would represent a waste of the many, varied skills already possessed by professionals and might impair the client's chance to receive help or even prevent it altogether. Obviously, it does not make sense for a worker to attempt to use a particular type of intervention with a client without fully understanding the purpose, aims, and objectives and without a knowledge and appreciation of the techniques it incorporates. Nor, on the other hand, does it mean that a worker, before attempting to help a client or patient with an alcohol problem, should mug up on every type of alcohol intervention available and be prepared to use any or all of them throughout the working relationship. There has to be some middle ground where the worker feels confident in his knowledge and sufficiently competent in terms of skills to use that knowledge for the benefit of the client or patient.

It will be helpful for each professional to find out where their individual middle ground lies. One way of doing this is to consider the main aims and objectives of their professional roles and to assess the skills they have developed in the course of their everyday work. The main work aim of most health and welfare professionals is to assist clients and/or patients experiencing a range of problems from physical or psychological difficulties through to social or legal ones. Some professional roles may also incorporate statutory or legal duties involving the protection of children or the supervision of clients on parole in the community. Whatever the particular professional role, the philosophy related to it will usually involve some or all of the following concepts:

— improving physical and/or psychological well-being
— encouraging responsibility for self and others
— facilitating non-problematic social functioning and interaction
— raising self-awareness
— improving the quality of life
— maximizing opportunities for self-management.

Basically, health and welfare professionals are in the business of helping other people by using a wide range of techniques and methods to achieve various goals, some of which are set by statutory or legal duties, and others which may be set between client and worker. Although overall aims of professionals' work may be similar, the objectives may differ according to the particular profession involved or type of problem under consideration.

When it comes to a question of skills, the similarities between different professions become even more evident. Apart from specialist, physical skills such as taking a blood-pressure reading, giving an injection, or delivering a baby, many professional workers' cognitive skills revolve around:

— giving information and/or advice
— assessing situations
— setting goals
— working within client/worker contracts
— monitoring and reviewing
— exploring alternatives

These skills may be employed in different contexts — on a one-to-one basis, within a family group or in a groupwork setting — but are often used to help a client confront a problem, explore its causes and effects, and consider and practise ways of overcoming it or limiting its problematic effects. The skills used and the helping processes involved are similar whether dealing with someone with coronary heart disease

45

or a sexual problem and are precisely the skills needed to help someone with an alcohol problem. In the case of the latter, outdated perceptions may lead both clients and workers to expect that for a successful outcome, some type of treatment needs to be administered. Treatment is often seen in the active sense of nursing someone or administering medication and yet such actions can only hope to tackle physical problems arising from alcohol misuse and alleviate the unpleasant side-effects of excess consumption.

Giving aspirin for hangovers and providing nursing care for those undergoing withdrawal is only part of the picture and there is still room for a lot of work to be done with the client or patient to help him modify his behaviour and make different health choices. Many people with drinking problems solve them alone or with the help and support of their immediate family and peer group, it is only a minority who come forward willingly or find themselves coerced into contact with a professional worker. It has been argued that 'the most likely difference between those who solve their difficulties without professional help and those who seek such help is likely to be in either the complexity of the problem or the availability of relevant resources' (Cartwright, 1985). In this case, resources refer to the psychological resources that may be possessed by the drinker such as knowledge, self-awareness, and interpersonal skills as well as the more commonly understood resources of money, a home, a job, and support from others. Cartwright suggests that it is the role of professionals involved in such situations to compensate for the psychological resources that may be lacking in the client, rather than trying to provide something new and different. In this way, he proposes that as there is a range of processes by which drinkers come to solve problems 'that these will be the same whether they occur in a treatment or community situation. The function of treatment is to facilitate those processes which have not evolved in the natural setting' Cartwright, 1985.

Health and welfare professionals should recognize that, whether dealing with coronary heart disease, sexual difficulties, or drinking problems, change is rarely simple or easy, nor is it usually accomplished overnight. Problems that have taken some time to develop will also take some time to be overcome and alcohol problems are no different in this respect. Just as an obese person can lose weight, however, or the stroke-affected person can learn to talk again, so the person experiencing drink problems can be encouraged to make changes that resolve the problems entirely or, at least, minimize their harmful effects. One of the most effective tools in this process is alcohol education.

Why and how should alcohol education fit into the workload?

Alcohol education should be seen as an on-going process that is intended to empower people to make their own decisions and choices based on accurate information. People receive information about alcohol and drinking behaviour all the time — much of it misleading — from friends, family, the media, and personal experience. There is very little formal education about alcohol and few attempts to redress the balance between misinformation and accurate information. Professional workers have a role to play in their relationships with clients or patients by:

— dispelling myths
— providing accurate information
— helping clients/patients determine where they stand and where they want to go
— exploring ways of modifying problematic behaviour
— identifying triggers that maintain problematic behaviour
— helping to set realistic goals
— helping to draw up a realistic timescale for change
— monitoring progress and helping to deal with relapse.

There are many overlaps between what are traditionally considered to be two distinct and separate activities of prevention and treatment. Marcus Grant 1979 proposes that, rather than being seen as separate activities, prevention and treatment should be seen as part of a continuum stretching from foetal alcohol syndrome FAS through to delirium tremens. He suggests that:

> There is no dividing line between prevention and treatment, except the reluctance (and, some would say, the competence) of practitioners of the one to become involved in dealing with the other. Indeed, increasingly, treatment approaches are coming to rely upon what might once have been thought of as preventive education, while prevention is coming to include self-monitoring techniques borrowed from the treatment area.
>
> (Grant 1979:90-1)

Alcohol education should be an integral part of the work of all health and welfare professionals and should range from prevention in its purest sense — stopping people from ever experiencing problems with alcohol — through to education, which enables the individual to understand the

47

risks involved and, if required, to modify his behaviour and adopt alternative ways of coping with problems. Professional workers, on reflection, may find that they have several opportunities for alcohol education and that they are often 'in the right place, at the right time'. They are frequently seen by clients as valid sources of information on issues relating to personal and family health and welfare and are often present during illness or a crisis situation. They have opportunities to develop mid- or long-term working relationships with clients and/or patients and may find education to empower clients and patients more personally satisfying than changing a dressing or discussing the payment of court fines.

Where does alcohol education fit in?

There is no single starting or concluding point for alcohol education when working with a client or patient and it is the responsibility of each worker to assess when to use alcohol education as part of a broad treatment programme, which techniques and approaches to include, and which goals and outcomes need to be achieved. If this does not sound particularly helpful or specific, it is because each client is different; the problems he presents with will vary as will his ability to respond in different ways. Accordingly, the alcohol-education component of any treatment programme will vary in emphasis, depth, and direction depending on the individual, the type of problems experienced, and the context in which they occur. Workers who are confident in their role and skills in alcohol education will be able to tailor their input to take account of these variables.

Some people will readily recognize that their drinking is getting out of control. They will have suffered too many interrupted nights' sleep followed by diarrhoea, stomach upsets, and lack of appetite the following morning to remain unaware of the links between their alcohol consumption and its after-effects. In response, they may promise themselves or their spouses or partners that they will cut down on their drinking, take more exercise, or get into work or home from work on time. Attempts at change may be made and, if successful, the problems associated with drinking will recede. If the attempts are not successful however, the drinker begins to lose self-esteem and confidence as does the spouse or partner and further attempts are either not seen as worthwhile or are abandoned altogether. A person in such a position needs alcohol education to help them know how and where to start making changes. They also need the encouragement and support of others — family, friends, the professional involved — to help them appreciate the progress being made and to feel better about themselves.

Other people are simply unaware of the impact of their drinking on their health, their relationships, and their work, or are so appalled at the thought of coping with life without alcohol, that they refuse to confront their drinking behaviour. These people will also benefit from alcohol education aimed at increasing knowledge of the effects of alcohol, raising self-awareness, and imparting skills in monitoring and controlling drinking behaviour. Again, outdated perceptions of what constitutes an alcoholic and the inevitable, irreversible deterioration caused by alcoholism, will affect both workers and clients alike. How many workers have heard clients re-assure them thus: 'I may have had a few drinks now and again but I am not an alcoholic'? It is as if there is a sudden cut-off point in drinking behaviour that delineates acceptable drinking and alcoholism. Those who see alcohol problems from this perspective, and who often equate alcoholism with homelessness or the loss of everything except the desire to drink, do not recognize that there are degrees of drinking, that heavy drinking may be short- or long-term, and that change can usually be effected for the better.

In terms of alcohol education, it may be helpful to imagine drinking as the bus journey that is set out in Figure 4.1. Anyone who has ever had an alcoholic drink has got onto the alcohol bus. Depending on their experience with their first alcoholic drink, they may decide not to make the journey at all and get off the bus straight away. Alternatively, they may travel along the route and get off the bus at the first bus stop, at moderate, social drinking. Education at this point would involve giving information about units of alcohol, blood-alcohol levels, topping up and patterns of sensible drinking. It might also include raising awareness of low and non-alcoholic drinks and the effects of peer-group pressure and round-buying. Some people might travel on to the second bus stop and might alight at the heavy-drinking stage. Here, education would include what had gone before with added emphasis on the widespread harmful effects of excessive consumption. It could also include strategies for monitoring and cutting down on consumption. Most people will either remain at one of these two stops or will journey up and down between them, increasing their alcohol consumption in response to certain situa-tions and decreasing it in response to others. As highlighted earlier, many people are able to resolve their own alcohol-related difficulties without having recourse to a professional worker. It is also important to note that in doing so, they belie the old concept of the inevitable 'slippery slope to ruin'.

Figure 4.1 The alcohol bus and its route

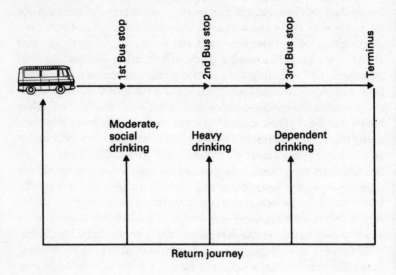

However, certain people will continue on the journey to alight at the dependent-drinking stage or may even continue all the way to the terminus. At this point, although health and welfare problems may be the most prevalent and may necessitate intervention in treatment terms, there will still be a role for alcohol education to increase knowledge, to help clients cope with the effects of withdrawal, and to encourage them to change their life styles. No-one is advocating that a brief, factual talk on alcohol would either constitute alcohol education or would be relevant to the homeless drinker but rather that, in working at a professional level with clients, there is always a role for alcohol education to enable the individual to eliminate or minimize problems and to help him achieve a better quality of life. A final point to note about Figure 4.1. is that, as with any bus trip, a return journey can always be made!

Most professional workers are aware of the advantages of early intervention in helping to minimize the harmful effects of heavy or dependent drinking. In its latest report, the Special Committee of the Royal College of Psychiatrists highlights the advantages of helping problem drinkers before they become severely dependent or have lost their social networks or prospects of employment.

It has been demonstrated that in these early cases clear unequivocal advice given in a non-judgemental manner, which helps the excessive drinker weigh up the advantages and disadvantages of his life style, has a discernible benefit, possibly over several years, if the brief contact is repeated.

(Royal College of Psychiatrists 1986:168–9)

Figure 4.2 Typical distribution of different levels of alcohol consumption in a population

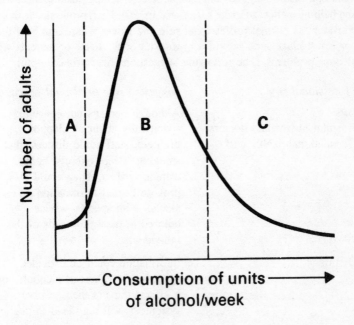

Source: New Report of a Special Committee of the Royal College of Psychiatrists (1986).
Note: A — Teetotallers or occasional drinkers; B — Moderate drinkers; C — Heavy or excessive drinkers.

The report goes on to bolster the role of professionals in alcohol education by stating that 'most harmful effects of drinking are not accounted for by that relatively small number of severely dependent people to whom the treatment services are directed, but by moderate and heavy drinkers'. Figure 4.2 details the distribution of alcohol consumption in a population and should help workers realize that there are opportunities for education with moderate and heavy drinkers. If such opportunities are used appropriately, they could have a greater impact on the community, in terms of reduced health problems and fewer road accidents, than interventions directed solely at severely dependent drinkers.

As already stated, although professionals may work in different contexts — within families or groups, in prisons or on a one-to-one basis — the skills needed for alcohol education are the same, although a slightly different approach may be needed depending on the particular context. Ewles and Simnett 1985 identify various activities involved in education including 'instructing, advising, explaining, listening, leading discussion and helping a client to make a decision' (p. 20). Each professional should consider his normal professional role and assess where and how they could introduce such activities in working with clients or patients with alcohol problems. The following suggestions may prove helpful:

Professional role	*Suggested role in alcohol education*
GPs Hospital nurses and doctors Occupational-health staff	Although perhaps not consulted specifically about an alcohol problem, staff could discuss: diet, smoking, sleep, exercise, and drinking habits. They could also provide factual information on alcohol with specific advice tailored to meet the needs of the individual.
Dietitians	Information could be provided on the calorific values of alcohol; how it affects/impairs the digestive system; how it may lead to peptic ulcers; how vitamin absorption may be impaired; the poor food value of alcohol.
Midwives	Care of the mother during pregnancy could include information about: the effects of alcohol on the foetus; the levels of safe drinking;

the effects of drunkenness or immoderate drinking during the first trimester; the link between alcohol consumption and spontaneous abortion.
Care of mother and baby after birth could include information on diet, sleep, relaxation and explanation of how drinking may affect the baby if mother breast feeds.

Probation officers
Social workers
Health visitors
Community nurses

Information could be provided on: the links between alcohol and crime, family dysfunction, and marital violence; the effects of excessive alcohol consumption on health, relationships, and child care; looking at alternative ways of coping and minimizing alcohol-related harm; raising awareness of 'game-playing' related to drinking behaviour; breaking cycles of behaviour; supporting and encouraging the drinker to change, as well as the spouse or partner and other family members.

Educating for change

Any individual who plans to go out into the 'real world' to try to influence others, change attitudes, and modify behaviour must be aware of the personal as well as the social consequences of such a decision:
'The psychologist can hardly do anything without realizing that for him the acquisition of knowledge opens up the most terrifying prospects of controlling what people do and how they think and how they behave and how they feel' J. Robert Oppenheimer.

(Zimbardo, Ebesen, and Maslach 1977:233)

Such statements reflect some of the internal doubts and uncertainties of professional workers who are confronted with their potential role as agents of individual change. Few people working in helping agencies would care to admit openly that, for them, the rewards of the job include an opportunity to control or direct clients' knowledge, attitudes, and behaviour and yet, for many, such a role is dictated by the statutory or legal requirements of their employing agency. The safety net lies in the fact that it is not — or should not be — the individual worker who determines what a client ought to know or how he should feel or behave but, rather, that the broad boundaries of appropriate, acceptable behaviour and attitudes are set by society and reinforced by both legislature and social norms. The boundaries are sufficiently wide to encompass diversity of thought, opinion, or behaviour but are also clearly marked so that if transgressed, sanctions may be applied.

In the case of alcohol, western society generally accepts that some people decry alcohol and never drink at all whereas others find it a wonderful beverage and wholeheartedly indulge whenever possible. The vast majority of drinkers lie somewhere between the two extremes. Sanctions will be applied, however, to individuals or groups that transgress these boundaries and those who not only feel that it is right to drink as much as possible from dawn to dusk but actually do so in reality, run the risk of being ostracized or rejected entirely as a result of their transgressions.

In educating for change, it is vitally important for workers to set the right climate and to work closely with clients or patients so that the desired changes do not originate solely from the employing agency, the individual worker, or his client or patient but are determined by and pursued in the interests of all three. Before using alcohol education to effect change in clients' or patients' knowledge, attitudes, or skills, workers should draw up their own goals and plan of action and should examine closely their own motivation and reasoning. This is only the first stage in the process and should be based on the steps highlighted in Table 4.1 (p. 55). The second, equally important step, is to encourage the client or patient, as far as is applicable, to follow the same process to elicit the changes he is seeking and is prepared to work towards. In this contract-making process the most important stage is for both worker and client to compare their answers with a view to deciding on changes which are desirable, realistic, and achievable on both sides. Obviously, this will involve a degree of compromise from both parties but will result in an agreed plan of action in which both will have a sense of direction and ownership.

Central to any program of change is a statement of the goals or specific behavioural objectives, a catalogue of potentially useful techniques to implement these goals, and a means of evaluating the success of the techniques and the entire action program.

(Zimbardo, Ebbeson and Maslach 1977:221)

Table 4.1 Setting the climate for change

1. Specify and state your own goals
   Think about what you would like your client/patient to know, feel and do.

   Knowledge — what do they know about alcohol?
                — what do they need to know?
                — is their knowledge accurate or based on misinformation, myths, or cultural beliefs?

   Attitudes — do they have a positive/negative attitude towards themselves?
              — do they have a positive/negative attitude to alcohol?
              — are attitudes based on personal self-esteem?

   Skills   — what skills do they have in relation to alcohol?
               — what skills are they lacking?
               — what skills could be improved upon?

2. Break your goals down into subgoals
   Almost any general goal can be broken down into specific subgoals. This will clarify what you want to achieve and will provide small, measurable units of change that can be ticked off as they are achieved.
   Change can be seen as a daunting, painful process. If small achievements are marked along the way, it will reinforce the sense of progress and accomplishment.

3. Look at the short- and long-term implications
   It is often easier to identify and achieve short-term changes but the longer term implications should also be considered.

   A drinker reducing his heavy-alcohol consumption to safer, harm-free levels may find he has more time to fill, more money available, a greater sense of well-being, and a desire to take part again in employment, a relationship, or family life. Although apparently positive spin-offs, there are also longer-term implications for social and emotional welfare. How will time be restructured, what will take the place of drinking?

4. Assess resources
   This involves both your resources and those of your client or patient and may involve concepts such as time, enthusiasm, commitment, and outside support.

5. Develop rapport with your client or patient
   Again this is a two-way process that involves listening, sharing, responding, and rewarding. (See Chapter 7 on communicating effectively.) It also requires an understanding and acceptance of the client's/patient's values and life style and commitment to the process of change in the form of shared ownership and responsibility.

6. Be prepared to change or compromise
At the first attempt, it may seem that you want to achieve and what your client or patient wants to achieve are fairly incompatible (see Table 4.2). Change and compromise will be needed on both sides to ensure that the process does not simply end in stalemate. A negotiated compromise is a more satisfactory outcome than a no-win situation.

7. Explore 'danger spots' in advance
Any programme aimed at modifying an individual's attitudes or behaviour will have various 'danger spots' or times when the individual is likely to revert back to the original attitude or behaviour because it is better known, feels more comfortable, or brings known rewards or payoffs. Rather than ignore potential danger spots, it is better to identify and confront them in advance and explore alternatives.

Danger spots could include some of the following:

Habit: 'I've always gone to the club on four nights a week.'
'I've always had a large sherry when I've got the children off to bed.'

Influence of peers/family: 'They bought me the drinks and I didn't like to refuse.'
'They said a couple of drinks wouldn't do any harm.'

Drug effect: 'I'd had a few drinks by then, so it was pointless to call it a day.'
'I was so drunk, I can't really remember what I did.'

Lack of alternatives: 'I had an hour to kill, so I went to the pub for a couple of drinks.'
'I'm so bored, it helps to while away the time.'
'There's nothing else worth doing.'

Longer-term implications: 'I cut down on my drinking and thought my wife would
(See point 3.)   be pleased. Instead, she doesn't want to know. I may as well drink.'

8. Reinforce the next contact
Having set a climate for change and agreed on goals and an appropriate course of action, offer further support by reinforcing the next point of contact. Discuss what can be achieved by that time and agree to review progress and discuss difficulties.

Table 4.2 First attempt at comparing priorities for knowledge, attitudes, and skills

	Client's/ patient's perspective	Worker's perspective
Knowledge	I want to know how I am going to pay the rent	I want him to know how to budget successfully
Attitudes	Alcohol is a good friend, it is a refuge, it helps me to cope	With alcohol there is always a price to pay. It is not the only way of coping
Skills	I want to be able to drink without all the upset and problems it causes within the family	I want him to be able to recognize the effects of his drinking on the family and to modify his behaviour

Discussion and compromise will be needed to bring the two differing perspectives closer together.

Alcohol education: getting down to it

Chapter five

Approaches to alcohol education

Just as a carpenter will use different tools to do different jobs or achieve varying effects, so a professional worker can use different approaches to alcohol education. It is easy to offer such advice as, 'I think it would be best for you to cut down on your drinking' or 'It would make most sense for you to give up drinking altogether' but, unless ways of achieving this are explored and the client's/patient's commitment to and belief in a course of action gained, the advice is likely to go unheeded. This is where alcohol education has a major role to play in helping the client/patient to become better informed, encouraging him to explore and understand his attitudes towards alcohol, and in equipping him to take decisions and act on them.

Over the last 20 years, the debate concerning appropriate behaviour goals for people with alcohol problems has increased. At one stage it was thought that the only way to help people get over such problems and prevent them from recurring was to help them stop drinking altogether. The self-help group, Alcoholics Anonymous has helped hundreds of thousands of people to achieve this goal by encouraging members to take only one day at a time and by offering emotional support through its group structure. One of AA's official publications states:

> We alcoholics are men and women who have lost the ability to control our drinking. We know that no real alcoholic *ever* gains control. All of us felt at times that we were regaining control . . . but we are convinced to a man that alcoholics of our type are in the grip of a progressive illness. Over any period of time we get worse, never better. . . . Physicians who are familiar with alcoholism agree that there is no such thing as making a normal drinker out of an alcoholic.

> (Alcoholics Anonymous 1955)

If this view of alcohol problems was accepted, then it would indeed appear that the only way to overcome such problems would be to give up drinking forever. It would also mean, however, accepting lack of control over one's life forever, and that, in spite of years and years of sobriety, acknowledging and *believing* that one drink would be sufficient to trigger a return to alcoholism. While not denying the validity of this philosophy, which has helped many people whose drinking had become highly damaging or even life-threatening to lead sober lives, working in an alcohol agency, I found it extremely sad to hear AA members discussing how they would react if offered sherry trifle!

As the definitions of alcoholism, however, have moved away from illness and disease towards learned, functional behaviour, the terms alcoholic and alcoholism have been replaced, for some, by problem drinker problematic drinking, and alcohol-related problems. Alternative behavioural goals for drinkers have also been explored and the suggestion put forward that some drinkers — previously considered alcoholic — may be able to return to social drinking. Claude Steiner upset more than one abstinence-oriented agency in the 1970s when he said:

> Alcoholism is not incurable. It is an acquired condition different from person to person, based partly on social pressure to drink, and partly on the emotional thinking and nutritional habits of the alcoholic. Alcoholism can be healed, and a few former alcoholics are evidently able to return to normal drinking though the majority either can't or won't.

> (Steiner 1979:195)

In the course of his work Steiner recognized that many drinkers involved in therapy who had remained sober for a year were keen to test their ability to drink socially. In the main, he found they fell into three distinct groupings. Those in the first group, when reintroduced to alcohol, lost control immediately and went back to harmful drinking. The second group found that, bit by bit, consumption increased along with involvement with alcohol. Members of this group decided not to continue drinking and were able to stop 'without incident or harmful aftereffects' (p. 35). People in the third group — which was also the smallest — found that they had regained control over their drinking, that alcohol was no longer an obsession and that they could 'simply take an occasional, enjoyable, social drink without any dire consequences' (p. 35).

Since then many other practitioners from the alcohol field have debated whether or not people who have lost all control over their drinking are able, after therapy, to return to social drinking and as many research papers have been published supporting the argument as those that refute it. Where does this leave the professional worker? In all likelihood he will be left feeling confused and wondering who is right and who is wrong. As in many aspects of human behaviour however, there is no right or wrong, no absolutes on which to construe practice from theory. Just as there are varying degrees of alcohol problems, so there are various possible responses and behaviour outcomes. If a young boy constantly gets into trouble through heavy drinking associated with attending football matches, it does not necessarily mean that he will have to give up alcohol (or football matches) altogether! Rather than professional workers deciding in advance which of Steiner's three groupings clients or patients might belong to, it would be more helpful and effective to begin with the individual in question and see what they want to achieve and what they feel is realistic and possible. As we saw in Chapter 4, mismatches in priorities are quite likely at this stage and final goals should be worked out and agreed by both the worker and client/patient. As a broad guideline, it will be helpful to:

1. *gather information about the drinking behaviour.*
   Is it binge or episodic drinking related to certain circumstances or triggered by certain situations?
   Is it excessive or heavy drinking which has continued and (possibly) increased over a period of time?
   Is it dependent drinking where the client/patient has become physically and/or psychologically dependent on alcohol?

2. *assess the presenting and underlying problems.*
   Are they medical or physical?
   Do they involve relationships and/or social situations?
   Are they related to the client's/patient's self-concept?
   Are they linked to the client's/patient's living circumstances or environment i.e. housing, education, employment?
   Do they involve breaking the law?

3. *discuss and agree goals with the client/patient.*
   Depending on the circumstances, behavioural goals related to alcohol consumption might include:

   (a) total abstinence;

(b) a period of abstinence followed by controlled drinking;

(c) reduction of consumption to controlled levels.

(As pointed out in Chapter 4, there will also be many subgoals involving knowledge, attitudes, and skills to be achieved that will help to mark progress towards behaviour change.)

4. *agree on and set a contract*.
This involves setting a realistic timescale, acknowledging possible difficulties, and discussing what happens if things go wrong and the progress anticipated is not made.

5. *monitor and review the contract*.
This helps to provide measurable units of change, takes account of progress or lack or it, and allows for flexibility in view of this.

Once the worker and the client/patient have undergone this process, both parties will have a much clearer idea of the plan of action and the time-scale within which it is to be achieved. It is unlikely that this point will be reached in the course of one meeting or interview. It may take several meetings to develop rapport with the client/patient (see Chapter 7), to explore their attitudes and feelings and to set jointly agreed goals. Once agreement has been reached however, the worker should assess how and where alcohol education can be used to help achieve the given goals. The next chapter gives specific details on how to plan alcohol education, but an appreciation is needed of the range of possible approaches to alcohol education and their strengths and limitations. Some of the main approaches are set out below and then applied to the original framework of knowledge, attitudes, and skills discussed in Chapter 4.

The range of approaches to alcohol education

Some of the main approaches to alcohol education include the information-giving, shock-horror, affective, situational, behavioural, and harm-minimization approaches. Most people find that effective alcohol education programmes are not based on a single approach, but take one or two components from each approach according to the goals that are being pursued. For example, if the main strength of the information-giving approach is that it helps to increase knowledge, a worker will have to incorporate another approach in his alcohol education if he wants to explore attitudes as well as to increase knowledge. In encouraging clients/patients to take charge of and accept responsibility for their own behaviour however, it is essential to begin with the individuals and to develop their skills and knowledge rather than attempting to impose predetermined goals. Also, as clients/patients do not exist in isolation, it is important, in the course of alcohol education, to acknowledge and involve others such as peers or family members who might help or hinder progress (see Chapter 8).

The information-giving approach

This concentrates on providing information and increasing knowledge. It could involve:

— dispelling myths and fallacies about alcohol
— teaching about the effects of alcohol, both short- and long-term
— information on units of alcohol, the topping-up process, and blood-alcohol levels
— information on alcohol and the law, especially drinking and driving.

The approach is based on the belief that human behaviour is rational and that increased knowledge will lead to changed behaviour. Research has shown this to be untrue and that the approach will only be successful in terms of increasing knowledge and is not likely to affect or change behaviour. As Marcus Grant points out 'knowledge, even relevant knowledge, does not carry instructions for its application' (Grant 1982:181).

The shock-horror approach

A further component of the information-giving approach involves shock-horror or attempting to deter people from a given behaviour by appealing to their fear of the outcome. Although used widely in the 1960s in relation to smoking and drug education, its use in relation to alcohol education has been limited for two reasons. Firstly, society as a whole accepts, and in many cases condones, the use of alcohol and it is difficult to sustain a shock-horror approach to a behaviour that is so common and entrenched. Secondly, there is no clear-cut message with regard to drinking alcohol as there is in the case of smoking cigarettes. It would be wrong to state that 'alcohol kills' as there are obviously many people leading happy, healthy lives who enjoy drinking alcohol. There are too many qualifications to be made in terms of the quantity, frequency, and circumstances of alcohol consumption for a strong shock-horror message to be formulated. In addition, research into the use of this approach has shown that 'in most cases high fear appeals *do not work* and can, in fact, have the *opposite* effect to that intended' (Howe and Wright 1987:158). If the alcohol-education message is disproved by reality, Stuteville has observed that the message may be entirely rejected and that the educator risks losing his credibility (Stuteville 1970;39–45).

The affective approach

The main focus of this approach is to consider the attitudes, opinions, and values held by the individual with regard to alcohol and to clarify them. It helps to draw out, from both the worker and the client/patient, areas of concern and to examine these with a view to modification or change. Again it assumes that by clarifying attitudes and raising levels of self-awareness, changes in behaviour will automatically ensue. Research shows that this approach is helpful in clarifying attitudes but that used in isolation, it is only one step towards modifying or changing behaviour. Applied to drinking behaviour, the approach could be used to explore:

how the client/patient feels about his drinking

the functional role it plays in his life

the problems that it causes

who is affected by the problems

the degree of responsibility and/or control that he feels.

The situational approach

As stated in Chapter 3, p. 31–3 the context in which drinking takes place is important and is likely to influence the type of drinking behaviour shown. For example, most people invited to their employer's home for a meal would aim to limit their alcohol consumption to two or three drinks, whereas drinking at an office Christmas party is less likely to be so constrained. The situational approach concentrates on the knowledge and skills needed to cope sensibly with various drinking situations, and can be used with clients/patients wishing to stop drinking altogether as well as those who wish to reduce their consumption and regain control of their drinking. Used by agencies such as Drinkwatchers* in their work with clients, the approach could involve increasing individuals' knowledge and skills in the following situations:

— refusing the offer of a drink
— avoiding getting drawn into round-buying
— stating a preference for a low- or non-alcoholic drink
— avoiding drinking at inappropriate times such as during the working day or when expected to drive a car
— limiting alcohol consumption on occasions when drinking is expected (parties, celebrations, Christmas, New Year).

The behavioural approach

Ewles and Simnett (1985:30) summed up 'The aim of this approach is to change people's attitudes and behaviour so that they adopt a "healthy" life-style'. Assuming that alcohol use is a learned, functional behaviour, the approach seeks to encourage people to adopt different, less harmful forms of behaviour by increasing their self-esteem and social competence. It includes increasing assertiveness and raising an individual's personal sense of control, confidence, and coping abilities. In health education in general, research has shown the approach to have varying degrees of effectiveness according to the behaviour in question but it has also been criticized for being manipulative. It risks inducing a sense of guilt or even rebelliousness in the client who, for whatever reasons, is unable to adopt the 'healthier' behaviour. It focuses attention on the individual and tends to neglect the wider influences on his drinking such as the immediate environment and, in the case of alcohol, it may involve the imposition of medical values on the individual.

> For example, losing weight and lowering blood pressure may be the most important thing to a doctor, but drinking beer in the pub with friends may be far more important to his overweight, middle-aged, unemployed patient. Who is to say which set of values is 'right' — the doctor or his patient? Whose life is it anyway?
>
> (Ewles and Simnett 1985:32)

*For further information about the national network of Drinkwatchers Groups contact: ACCEPT Clinic, 200 Seagrave Road, London SW6 IRQ. Tel. 01-381 3155

Again, the importance of working from the client's/patient's point of view must be stressed along with the need to work out and agree behavioural goals jointly rather than coercing the client/patient to adopt behaviour considered to be 'correct and healthy' by the professional worker alone.

The harm minimization approach

Although not an entirely new approach in itself, alcohol education based on harm minimization selects specific goals from the other approaches already covered. It does not aim to stop people from drinking altogether, but rather to reduce or minimize their harmful patterns of drinking. To use this approach effectively, both clients/patients and professional workers need to be aware of the patterns of drinking behaviour and the types of problems they give rise to. This can be achieved by using some of the strategies detailed in Chapter 7, particularly the balance sheet of drinking, the drinker's diary, and the diary of troublesome/troublefree drinking. Having highlighted times and circumstances when alcohol consumption is likely to give rise to problems, the approach seeks to minimize the problems by:

— exploring alternatives to drinking
— encouraging controlled drinking in given situations
— raising awareness of the effects of certain circumstances and contexts on drinking behaviour
— helping the drinker to minimize resulting problems that may affect himself and other people.

These constitute some of the main approaches to alcohol education and, through practice, each professional will discover the approach that feels most comfortable and appears to be the most relevant according to particular circumstances. Some professionals may find at first that they are constrained by the limitations of their professional role. For instance, in the example given about the doctor and his patient in the behavioural approach p. 67, the doctor, because of his professional role, must stress the importance of reducing alcohol consumption if his patient is to lose weight and reduce his blood pressure. The patient, however, may have other ideas about losing weight and lowering blood pressure by dieting and taking more exercise. The doctor should acknowledge these ideas and, if appropriate, support the patient in them while continuing to highlight the links between excessive alcohol consumption and obesity and hypertension. In this way, neither the patient's nor the doctor's views are ignored or compromised.

If we return to the framework of knowledge, attitudes, and skills set out in Chapter 4, Table 5.1 puts forward some suggested goals under each heading, indicates which approach (or approaches) might be used, and assesses their strengths and limitations.

Table 5.1 Choosing an educational approach

Knowledge

You want to
— increase your client's knowledge of the effects of alcohol
— dispel myths about alcohol
— encourage him to recognize low/high-risk levels of consumption
— help him add up his own levels of consumption

Approach: An educational, information-giving approach to provide facts, to help the client/patient discover things for himself and to ensure better understanding

Pros	*Cons*
Provides a sound information base for decision-making	Information may not be acted on
Empowers client/patient	Learning may not be related to behaviour

Attitudes

You want your client/patient
— to feel responsible for his own drinking and behaviour
— to feel in control of his drinking
— to feel confident in his own skills and abilities
— to feel that there are other rewards or ways of coping

Approach: A client-centred, affective aproach that explores and clarifies values and attitudes rather than seeking to impose them

Pros	*Cons*
Not value-laden or judgemental	Client may hold different or unhelpful attitudes to the worker
Client-directed and relevant	Client may prefer to be told what to do, how to feel and what to think
	Client may not apply modified attitudes to his behaviour

	Skills
You want to teach your client/patient	— to monitor his drinking
	— to practise strategies for controlling consumption
	— to deal successfully with peer/family pressure
	— to develop skills in assessing the benefits and drawbacks of certain behaviours
	— to take decisions and act on them

Approach: A behavioural and/or situational approach in which appropriate skills are identified, practised and put into action

Pros	*Cons*
Empowers client and enables him to take charge	Client may use skills to achieve 'undesirable' outcomes

Day-to-day education and special inputs

By now it is hoped that readers will have developed a personal rationale for including alcohol education in their day-to-day work with clients and will appreciate the broad range of approaches to alcohol education and their individual strengths and limitations. Many professionals work on a one-to-one basis with their clients or patients, although some will be involved with family or self-help groups and yet others will be invited (or expected!) to give special educational inputs to certain groups. The skills needed to work on a one-to-one basis or in groups are largely the same although the emphasis might be slightly different. The process by which alcohol education is planned, implemented, and monitored remains the same whatever the situation (see Chapter 6).

Although it is beyond the scope of this book to consider the skills needed for groupwork in great depth, consideration of the following points will help workers feel prepared and confident when asked to undertake alcohol education in a groupwork setting. Many people feel nervous when asked to give a formal talk to a group or to run a group session and find that adequate preparation helps to reduce that feeling of nervousness.

Start with the group

Just as alcohol education on a one-to-one basis begins with the individual, so a formal presentation or groupwork session should acknowledge the group members. Find out as much as you can about the group in advance — what do people already know? what are they expecting to cover? — and incorporate this information into your planning process (see Chapter 6).

Be prepared

You may benefit from making notes that will support your alcohol-education input or remind you of the issues you wish to introduce to the group. Do not feel embarrassed about referring to them. It shows the group that you hve done some preparation in advance and reminds them that there is a structure to the process that they are undergoing. A brief synopsis of your notes giving main headings and key points for each heading could also be used as a handout at the end of your session.

Preparation will also involve thinking about where you are going to implement the alcohol education. If possible, visit the venue in advance and check out the facilities it offers. If you intend to use audiovisual materials, make sure that there are sufficient power points, extension leads, and appropriate equipment available. Problems can arise with audiovisual equipment and the best way to ensure that everything is in good working order and compatible with the materials you intend to use is to take your own equipment. For some people however, this is simply not a practical option.

When I first began to work as an alcohol educator, I felt quite intimidated by requests for inputs to different groups and, partly to hide my anxieties and, partly because I felt I had a duty to 'entertain' my audience, I used to make extensive use of alcohol education videos and films. With plenty of advance preparation on my part, all went smoothly until the time I was asked to give an input on alcohol and young people to a women's group which met weekly at a local school. I decided on a short presentation that would include some facts and figures, followed by a film and intended to round the evening off with some questions and answers and a display of relevant books and leaflets. The women's group agreed to provide the film projector and screen.

Unfortunately the layout of the school was not well known to me and, although I had set off in good time, it took some time simply to find the room where we were to meet. The women were already assembled so I thought it would be best to launch straight into the planned presentation. After about 20 minutes, I began to wind up and my heart sank as three volunteers brought in the screen and film projector. The screen, which was a paper one, should have unwound smoothly from its box but split from top to bottom as two ladies tried to erect it. Meanwhile, I struggled with the film projector (which looked as if it had come out of the Ark) and, due to nervousness and unfamiliarity with the equipment, managed to shred six feet of lead-in tape and only just succeeded in stopping the machine gobbling up the film altogether. I realized the situation was hopeless and apologized to the group for the lack of film. They took it in good part, however, and used the next hour and a half to ask questions and raise issues that were of particular relevance to them. For me, the session passed by in a flash and I understood that it is more important to involve group members in their own learning than to attempt to 'entertain' them or to fill in time with a film or video.

Arrive in good time

For the previous reasons, always try to arrive in good time so that you can set the room up as you want — arrange seating, familiarize yourself with equipment and light switches — and order your notes and lay out any books, leaflets, or handouts in advance.

Vary the pace

Having decided what you want to put across to the group or what you want them to consider, remember to vary the pace of what you do. If people are not to lose their concentration, it is best to restrict formal inputs to 10–20 minutes and to include other activities that will involve group members such as brainstorming, discussion, and work in pairs or small groups.

Obtain feedback

Without appearing to fish for compliments, it is important to elicit feedback from the group! Different ways of achieving this are suggested in Chapter 6.

Education as a caring activity

Traditionally, caring for a client or patient in a professional working relationship has involved the notion of doing things for people in the positive sense. It is relatively easy to give good advice, change a dressing, or administer medication but more difficult to enable a client or patient to make changes for himself and encourage him to try out new skills and alternative ways of coping. In Chapter 7 we look at the skills needed to establish a good working relationship with clients and patients, but at this point it is worthwhile considering how alcohol education can be seen as a caring activity.

In Chapter 2, p. 23 the results of a study of alcohol abusers who had attended therapy sessions at the Mount Zeehan Alcohol Treatment Unit in Canterbury were highlighted. They showed that the quality of the relationship established with the professional worker, being given factual information relating to problems, and being enabled to see life from a different perspective were considered to be some of the most helpful, therapeutic experiences. In his chapter entitled '*Is treatment an effective way of helping clients?*' Cartwright (1985:131–3) explains that 'the most important element in effecting therapeutic change is the alcohol abuser's experience of being in a "therapeutically committed" relationship'. He emphasizes the importance of the professional worker feeling secure in his therapeutic role and developing an empathetic relationship with the drinker and says 'because alcohol abusers are so often at the centre of relationships marked by mistrust, misunderstanding and conflict, these qualities may be even more important with this client group than with others.'

Alcohol education has a major role to play in the development of such a relationship as it should, if properly planned, begin with the drinker himself — recognize his level of knowledge and explore his values, attitudes and opinions. It should go on to help him recognize how his behaviour affects others and enable him to take responsibility for his actions by increasing his skills and his abilities to use alternative coping strategies. It is an empowering, enabling process that helps clients and patients to take charge of their own lives and to exercise a degree of control over their drinking that feels appropriate to them.

Chapter six

Planning alcohol education

This chapter offers a straightforward planning process that will help to ensure appropriate matching of goals, content, and method, a smooth delivery, and evaluation of the effect of the input on alcohol education. The process can be used whether you are planning to work on a one-to-basis with a client or patient or in a groupwork setting. At first glance it seems that there are a lot of steps to be taken before implementing the education with your client/patient or group but you will probably find that, without acknowledging it consciously, you already undertake many of them when preparing work with a client or group. Table 6.1 provides a brief summary of the necessary steps in the planning process and is transferable to education about any other health topic such as diet, smoking, or exercise. Planning your alcohol education will help you to move away from simply giving information or advice (although both will have a part to play) and will allow you to make use of the approaches highlighted in the last chapter. By setting goals, you provide an opportunity to measure progress that will be helpful to both you and your client/patient or group and you are encouraged to identify and make best use of the resources around you. Evaluation will not only help to highlight progress, but will also throw up any weak spots or areas that need further attention.

The planning process

This model is based on Howe and Wright 1987:173–84)

Step 1: Identify your target group

The first step in planning is to identify who you intend to educate. Is

Table 6.1 Planning alcohol education

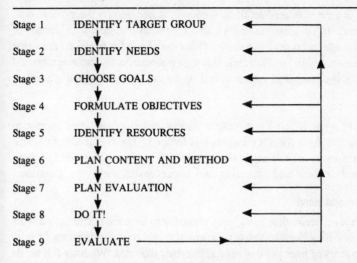

Stage 1	IDENTIFY TARGET GROUP
Stage 2	IDENTIFY NEEDS
Stage 3	CHOOSE GOALS
Stage 4	FORMULATE OBJECTIVES
Stage 5	IDENTIFY RESOURCES
Stage 6	PLAN CONTENT AND METHOD
Stage 7	PLAN EVALUATION
Stage 8	DO IT!
Stage 9	EVALUATE

This scheme applies equally to work at the one-to-one level and with groups.
Some of the details are clearly not appropriate, but the principles remain the same.
Use the results of evaluation to amend and improve future plans

Source: Howe and Wright, 1987.

it the client or patient, will it involve family members and/or peers, or
is it a group of individuals?
What is their knowledge and experience of alcohol? Is it positive or
problem based, does it involve any particular health problems that may
need attention?
What is the level of ability? Might there be difficulties with age, level
of understanding, culture or language?

Step 2: Identify the alcohol-education needs

It is easy to state generally that 'my client/patient needs to know this'
or 'my group needs to be able to perform that skill'. If clients are to
be encouraged however, to take responsiblity for themselves, it will be
helpful to explore the kinds of need that there are and see which ones
apply to your target group. Do not forget to acknowledge your own needs
as well. There are four kinds of need: normative, felt, expressed, and
comparative.

Normative need

This is a need related to alcohol education decided by the professional worker. It is what he thinks the client/patient needs in terms of knowledge, attitudes, and skills. This type of need is based on the value judgements of the worker and, although not necessarily incorrect, should always be compared and matched up to the client's/patient's needs.

Felt need

This is what is felt by the client/patient and may, at first, appear to contradict the worker's thoughts and feelings. The felt needs of clients/patients may, in such cases, be limited by their levels of knowledge about alcohol or their understanding and awareness of their own situation.

Expressed need

These are needs that have been turned into demands. Clients/patients may say they need to know how to cut down on their drinking or how three pints of beer per day may affect their diabetes. Whether felt needs are turned into expressed needs will depend on opportunity, motivation, and skills in assertiveness on the part of the individual or the group. Workers have a role to play in providing clients/patients with opportunity for an open expression of needs. This may also apply to family members and/or peers who may be involved in problems related to alcohol.

Comparative need

These needs are defined by comparing individual clients/patients or groups of clients/patients, some of whom have received alcohol education and some of whom have not. If a professional works with an individual on reducing his consumption of alcohol and looks at ways of monitoring and controlling it, it may be helpful to go through the same process with the spouse/partner so that she can play a supportive role and not feel left in the dark.

At this stage, it will also help to ask the question, 'Is alcohol education the answer to the need?' In all likelihood, where alcohol consumption has begun to cause problems, alcohol education will form only part of the response. Other influences such as social, health, economic, or legal factors may be at play and will need to be acknowledged. Alcohol education alone cannot be expected to solve all problems and meet all needs (see Table 6.2).

Table 6.2 Strengths and limitations of alcohol education

Strengths

Empowers the client/patient
Action plans are not just worker-directed
Encourages responsibility for self and others
Teaches skills that are transferable to other areas of life
Increases knowledge and raises levels of understanding
Modifies attitudes and behaviour
Can be satisfying for both worker and client/patient

Limitations

Other factors may be involved where alcohol education is not an appropriate response
May not have an immediate, noticeable effect
May need regular repetition and reinforcement
May require effort from client/patient
May not provide an immediate reward or payoff

Step 3: choose your goals

'Goal setting, in which the drinker should be actively participant, should not focus exclusively on drinking behaviour.' (Gwinner 1979: 115). Consider a wide range of goals — some of which will involve changes in knowledge, attitudes, or skills — and include goals that will help to reinforce changes once they have been made. There are many different goals to chose from and selection should involve both the worker and client/patient. The following are some suggestions:

Raising consciousness   —   about the role and function of alcohol in an individual's life;
  —   about the short/long-term effects of drinking behaviour.

Increasing knowledge   —   about the effects of alcohol on the body;
  —   about units of alcohol and safe-drinking levels.

Improving self-awareness   —   about feelings and attitudes towards drinking;
  —   of the benefits and drawbacks of different patterns of consumption.

Facilitating attitude change*	— looking at attitudes to moderate drinkers or drunkenness;
	— modifying feelings and values.
Encouraging decision-making	— combining knowledge and attitudes with decision-making skills;
	— practising making decisions.
Assisting behaviour change	— acting on the aforementioned and carrying it out;
	— assessing realistic opportunities to change behaviour;
	— providing regular feedback.

Step 4: Formulate your objectives

Objectives are generally defined in terms of knowledge, attitudes, beliefs, and behaviour. It will be helpful to decide what you want your client/patient or group to know, feel, and do as a result of your alcohol education. As far as possible, objectives should be discussed and agreed between the worker and the individual or group.

This lessens the risk of the worker imposing only his feelings, views, and attitudes on the situation and helps to ensure that the objectives agreed are both realistic and achievable for the individual or group. It is satisfying for both workers and their clients/patients to see progress being made but, if it is not, clearly defined objectives may show the areas that need improving.

Step 5: Identity resources — available and required

Many people think resources simply mean leaflets, books, posters, films, or videos and are unaware that there is a wider pool of resources available to the alcohol educator. The most important resource is *you* and what

---

*Attitudes may change as a result of a change in behaviour rather than before it. Attitude change may reinforce behaviour change (based on Reich and Adcock 1976). For example, a man who refuses to eat Italian, Chinese, or Indian food because he perceives it as 'foreign and unappetising', may only change his attitude after he has enjoyed pasta, chop suey, or curry. His change in behaviour leads to a change in attitude, which then reinforces the behaviour.

you can offer to the individual or group in terms of your knowledge, experience, skills, enthusiasm, energy, and time.

It is important not to ignore similar qualities that may be possessed by your client/patient or group. What do they know about drinking? What do their experiences relate to? What types of skills do they already have?

People who are in a position to influence the drinker should also be acknowledged. They may include an employer and colleagues, family members and relatives, or peers and friends. Are they able/willing to become involved, to take on a role or to be supportive?

Look around to see the resources that might be available to you, the professional worker. Does your manager support you? Will colleagues listen to you and discuss your work? Is there a local alcohol agency that could provide you with guidelines, information, or casework support? Could your local health-education unit provide material resources, which might include leaflets, posters, audiovisual aids, and equipment? Could health-education staff help with the skills needed to work with groups?

Step 6: Plan the content and method

There are many preconceived alcohol education programmes that tell you that you must include this aspect or that you must not neglect another aspect, but one omission that is frequently made relates to stated goals and objectives for such programmes.

At this stage you should be able to go back to the goals and objectives set by you *and* the individual or group to see what sort of alcohol-education content is indicated. Reconsider the various approaches to alcohol education highlighted in Chapter 5 and decide which you are going to use, or which mixture of components from different approaches seems most appropriate, given the circumstances within which you are working.

The methods you chose to use will also relate to the circumstances but may include some of the following:

giving information	teaching particular skills
reading leaflets/books	demonstrating/practising
brainstorming	role play/rehearsing situations with feedback
questions and answers	questionnaires

watching films/videos   keeping diaries

talking/listening   holding discussions

Step 7: Plan your evaluation

To help you assess whether the alcohol education has been helpful and
what impact it has made, it is important to chose a way to evaluate it.
The type of evaluation used will be indicated, to a large extent, by the
circumstances in which the education was carried out and the goals it
was intended to achieve. For example, if your alcohol-education input
was intended to inform members of a small group about units of alcohol
and absorption/elimination rates, the evaluation would be concerned with
changes in knowledge and whether or not they had understood. If the
input was also intended to enable them to monitor and modify their rate
of consumption, the evaluation would also be concerned with changes
in behaviour.

'There are two main types of evaluation; evaluation to measure
whether the intended outcomes were achieved (effectiveness) and evaluation to measure whether the most appropriate methods were used
(process)' (Howe and Wright 1987:196).

You could evaluate the effectiveness of your alcohol education by
looking for:

Changes in knowledge

Use tests, questionnaires, or quizzes. Ask clients/patients what they have
learned and how they might use their new knowledge.

Changes in consciousness

Is the client/patient thinking and talking about new issues or seeing things
from a different perspective? Have group members asked for more
information, a further input, or more leaflets?

Changes in self-awareness and attitudes

Have there been changes in what clients/patients say and do as a result
of your alcohol education? In groups, use questionnaires before and after
your input to see which changes have been made (see Table 6.3).

Decision-making skills

Ask clients/patients or group members which decisions they have made
and what they intend to do. If appropriate, ask them to write down their

decisions. It may be necessary to check that they are able to write. Some people go through life without being able to.

Changes in behaviour

If decisions are made and written down, observe whether they are acted upon. Do clients/patients or group members demonstrate new behaviour? Monitor and keep records of behaviour changes, i.e. encourage clients/patients to keep a 'drinker's diary' (see chapter 8).

Table 6.3 Self-awareness questionnaire to be completed before and after an alcohol education input

I believe that:	Very strongly	Strongly	Moderately	Not at all
Alcohol plays a part in my personal problems				
I can learn to control my alcohol consumption				
I am responsible for my own behaviour				
My drinking affects other people				

By looking at whether the methods you used for your alcohol education were appropriate,you could also evaluate the *process* as follows:

Self-evaluation

What do you feel you did well/badly? If you were to repeat the input, what would you change and do differently? Remember to balance what you did well with the more negative aspects and do not be so self-critical that you affect your self-confidence.

Peer-evaluation

If appropriate, you could ask a friend or colleague to observe your alcohol-education input and give you both positive comments and suggestions for improvement. Be sure to ask for both and not simply a list of things you did wrong. If you have spent time in planning your alcohol education, there should not be any glaring errors but possibly areas for improvement.

Client/patient evaluation

Ask for verbal feedback from clients/patients or group members. What did they like best or get the most from? What did they like least? Are their comments related to the methods you used as well as the content? What would they like to change?

In group settings it may be appropriate to use rounds to obtain feedback such as: 'One thing I liked was . . . and one thing I disliked was . . . ' and 'the best thing for me was . . . ' Alternatively you could ask for written feedback by using brief questionnaires (see Table 6.4).

Table 6.4 Evaluation questionnaire

During this session on alcohol education:

1. The thing I found most useful was . . .
2. I would like to know more about . . .
3. The way the session was run was . . .
4. If changes are made I would like to see . . .

Step 8: Action

Put your plans into action, remembering to carry out the evaluation you have chosen.

Step 9: Evaluate your alcohol education

Use the results of your evaluation to reassess each of the steps you took to plan your alcohol education (see Table 6.1). This should help to indicate where changes and improvements might be made. For example, if several group members say the thing they liked least was the selection of slides you showed, find another selection, use a film/video which gives the same information, or ask them what they would prefer instead.

If any individual client/patient indicates that he has found something unhelpful, always ask why. While working as an alcohol and drug counsellor, I found that a female client consistently came to our counselling appointment saying she had lost or forgotten her drinker's diary. I explained that it would be helpful to know the level and patterns of her drinking so that we could look at where reduction and changes could be made. After several weeks without completing a diary, she eventually admitted that she did not even want to try to fill one in because she was afraid of seeing the amount she drank written down. At face value, I could have accepted (mistakenly) that she simply found the drinker's diary unhelpful, but, by asking her to explain why, she told me her real reasons and we had to do a lot of work on overcoming her fears.

If your colleagues are involved in similar work, give them the benefit of your evaluation. You may find that they have experienced similar problems or have used different solutions and are prepared to share their experiences.

Chapter seven

Implementing alcohol education

A difficulty often cited by professional workers is that of actually
broaching the topic of alcohol with a client or patient. The worker may
suspect that alcohol is causing difficulties for a particular individual or
for a family, but is uncertain about how to bring the topic out into the
open. Above all, workers fear rejection and denial if they broach the
topic in a clumsy or obvious manner. From the client's/patient's point
of view, the situation may look slightly different. It could be that the
client/patient has been waiting for an appropriate moment at which to
bring fears, uncertainties, and problems relating to alcohol into the open
and that certain questions or inferences on the part of the worker provide
that opportunity and trigger the client's/patient's need to share and off-
load. Alternatively, the client/patient may view his drinking as a taboo
subject for discussion and may put up a good many barriers and obstacles
to prevent the worker getting through. Such barriers might include:

Outright denial	'There is nothing wrong at all, I feel fine,'
Avoiding or dismissing issues	'That all happened a month ago. I've forgotton all about it now. It's not worth discussing.'
Bringing in other topics	'It's not my drinking that bothers me. What really worries me is that I can't get to sleep at nights. It's driving me crazy,'
Using humour inappropriately:	'It's all a bit of a joke really. Well you've got to laugh, haven't you?'

Other ways of avoiding discussion of drinking behaviour include silence and apparent indifference or apathy. The worker literally feels as if he is up against a brick wall and, at this point, there is a risk of open, two-way communication degenerating into a battle of wills. The worker is determined that conversation will centre on the drinking behaviour, while the client/patient is equally determined that it will not. In this situation each is determined to win, sees the other as the opposition, and feels exposed to unwelcome manipulation. What should the worker do? If the subject of drinking has been brought up and has received a negative reaction from the client or patient, it is not appropriate to carry on regardless, ignoring what the client/patient is actually saying. Any attempt at alcohol education would be wasted because the climate is not right for discussion and rapport and a good working relationship have yet to be established between the worker and client/patient. At this point it is necessary to accept what the client says — it is no problem, it is a joke, my insomnia bothers me — and work with that to develop a better working relationship (see Table 7.1).

Table 7.1 Power relationships between workers and clients/patients

		Style of relationship	Probable effect
Client Patient	worker	Authoritarian/expert . . . . Worker-dominated (win-lose)	
		Client-centred . . . . Participatory power (win-win)	
		Permissive/collusive . . . . Client-dominated (lose-win)	

Establishing relationships

Establishing a working relationship with a client or patient means going beyond a discussion of the weather, the news, or whether to have a cup of tea or coffee, although these may be the first steps in the process. In Chapter 5 we saw how alcohol users' relationships may be marked by mistrust, misunderstanding, and conflict. It is essential to establish a degree of trust and rapport between the worker and the client/patient if progress is to be made. Changes made in relation to drinking behaviour can be seen as threatening and the client needs to know and feel that the support of the worker is there if he is to take risks and try out new things. The worker needs to use patience, humour, honesty, and understanding and may also be required to share something of himself. Obviously, sharing does not necessarily mean relating personal anecdotes or beginning every sentence with, 'When I was in that situation . . .'. Sharing involves being open with the client, showing that there are two people (at least) involved in the situation and that the client/patient is not simply seen as a problem case to be tackled by the professional worker. The worker should aim to have 'unconditional positive regard' for the client/patient, which includes offering him 'an outgoing positive feeling without reservation, without evaluation' (Rogers 1961:385). Basically, this means accepting the client/patient in a positive way without laying down imaginary conditions such as:

Degree of commitment	'She had better show she is motivated before I undertake any work with her.'
Adherence	'He'll have to do as I say or we're not going to get anywhere.'
Compliance	'The family will have to go along with what I've proposed if they expect any improvement.'

Conditions such as these held in the mind of the worker can act as effective barriers and obstacles to establishing a good working relationship. Even though they remain unstated, they may be sensed by the client/patient, who will not be encouraged to open up and explore sensitive areas. The following processes are all ways in which a working relationship can be established, deepened, and maintained.

Creating trust and rapport

Some people are naturally talented at creating a sense of rapport and intimacy and seem adept at saying the right thing at the right time and listening in the right places. Although such skills should certainly be seen as a bonus, they are not necessarily innate. They *can* be learned by others if they are prepared to work on a basis of mutual respect between worker and client/patient. Brandes and Ginnis point out that:

this sort of respect does not depend only on expertise; it depends upon human interaction characterised by trust and high regard. Neither is it dependent on the charisma of the leader [worker], but rather upon the leader's [worker's] skill in communication, and this can be learned.

(Brandes and Ginnis 1986:20–1)

Everyone, not just those who drink, has experienced problems and, to identify the criteria needed to create trust and rapport, it may be helpful to imagine you have a problem and list the things you would like from someone who is prepared to help you. Your list might include:

Smiling	Not judging
Listening to me	Not giving advice
Looking at me	Had time for me
Looked as if they could cope	Was not shocked
Encouraged me to feel I could change	Touched me
Showed confidence in me	

These are all basic skills in communication. Use them to help to create trust and rapport. Some aspects are now considered in more detail and examples are given.

Setting the climate for open discussion

The worker's role

When you first meet a client/patient is your facial expression pleasant and welcoming or do you tend to look serious or worried? First impressions do make an impact and, in a busy working day, it is worth taking a minute or two to mentally 'shelve' the last client, meeting, or problem and to prepare yourself to be open and receptive to the next client or patient.

It is also important to look someone in the eye from time to time as this indicates that you are interested in what they are saying and are attending. Unbroken eye contact over a length of time, however, can be seen as challenging or threatening, so it is helpful to vary it. It is quite normal and acceptable to look away from someone while you are thinking, interpreting information, or preparing to respond. A distressed client may, however, interpret this as you showing a lack of interest in what they are saying and may expect a lot of direct eye contact to reassure them in a difficult or crisis situation.

Other forms of non-verbal communication include posture, proximity, nodding, smiling, and touching. Adopting an open posture and leaning towards a client/patient show that you are interested and open to them. Leaning back with folded arms and crossed legs may indicate the opposite. Proximity and touch are also important in letting a client/patient know you are there and willing to offer reassurance although they should be used with caution. Sitting side by side is helpful if you are looking at literature or a drinker's diary together whereas sitting behind a desk or table can seem distant and official. A touch on the arm or hand when a client arrives, leaves, or appears distressed will convey your acceptance, friendliness, and support. While the client/patient is talking to you, he will find it encouraging if you nod and smile from time to time, showing that you are listening to and accepting what is said.

Workers would be wrong to imagine that they have to use all of these tactics or risk failing to establish a relationship! It is almost certain that you use many of them quite naturally already. Perhaps you should look at the tactics you seldom use and consider adding one or two to your repertoire.

The client's/patient's role

Although it would not be appropriate in the first instance to ask your client or patient to change their forms of non-verbal communication to make the task of creating trust and rapport easier, you can tell a lot about how a client/patient is feeling by observing their body movements.

Does your client/patient look bored, worried or shut off? Is he sitting well away from you with legs crossed? Is eye contact very limited? If so, this may indicate a degree of embarrassment or discomfort. Your client may not feel able to open up or may want to avoid engaging in any meaningful discussion with you. There is no instant remedy for this, but you should observe how the client is feeling and react by using some of the aforementioned tactics. If you continue in this manner, the client should, in time, feel confident enough to begin to talk freely.

Broaching the topic of drinking

Having set the climate for open discussion, how do you go about broaching the subject of alcohol and the client's/patient's drinking behaviour? If it is an early session, it is better to allow the client/patient to bring out for discussion what concerns him rather than attempting to home in on drinking problems straight away. Even if alcohol is fairly central to the picture, the worker will make a better assessment of the role it plays by obtaining as full a picture of the client's situation as possible. Harwin and Hunt say that there are three principles to helping the individual who is experiencing alcohol or alcohol-related problems:

> The first one requires the worker to establish the contribution of
> alcohol to the person's difficulties. In the second the helper
> works with the client to secure his co-operation. These two
> processes pave the way for the third, in which an offer of help is
> made and a variety of strategies are examined to determine
> which might be most effective.
>
> (Harwin and Hunt 1979:143–6)

Clients are unlikely to present a cohesive, composite picture of their situation without help from the worker. When involved in a problem on an emotional level, it is easy to allow things to get out of perspective and to misinterpret what is happening. The professional worker can help by using active listening and open questions to encourage the client to talk and by structuring and paraphrasing the conversation to help the client gain a better perspective of his situation.

Active listening

Listening skills are as important to alcohol education as teaching skills and, by using active listening, the worker will understand what the client/patient is saying and will also be able to communicate that understanding back to the client/patient. There is a good deal of difference between simply hearing words and actively listening to and reflecting the feelings and emotional content of what is said. Reflecting the feelings of the client/patient allows the worker to clarify uncertainties, to check that he has understood what the client/patient is saying and to reassure the client/patient that he is being both understood and accepted.

> A counsellor [worker] can reflect content by a short, simple re-statement or paraphrasing of the essence of what the client has actually said. Reflection of content condenses and crystallises in a fresh way the information a client gives. The counsellor [worker] can also reflect feeling, that part of the client's statement that represents the emotional message. Often what is said (content) does not communicate the real meaning. Reflection of feeling focuses on this underlying or unstated message.
>
> (Munro, Manthei and Small 1983:56)

Practice is needed to develop skills in active listening as it is a very demanding task requiring the worker's full attention. It is easy to allow attention to wander away from what the client/patient is saying and to begin to rehearse responses or to interpret what is being said. Other distractions to active listening include fidgeting, criticizing, agreeing, disagreeing, and interrupting as this means the worker is not concentrating fully on what the client/patient is saying. Using some of the following responses will help the worker check whether or not he has understood the client/patient and, if not, will allow the client/patient to correct the worker.

'You feel . . .

'Is what you're saying . . .?'

'You seem to be saying . . .'

'From your point of view . . .'

'You seem . . . Is that right?'

Readers will note the absence of the word 'I' in these responses. The client remains feeling important and central to the working relationship and is not told:

'I think your problem is . . .'

'I feel what you are really saying . . .'

'I know just how you feel . . .'

Which questions to use?

Some workers feel very uncomfortable about asking questions related to their client's or patient's drinking behaviour although they will happily ask whether the client is sleeping properly, if they are managing financially, or whether their relationship with their spouse or partner has improved. It is best to face such feelings and to try to work out what causes them, rather than resolving to ignore the topic of alcohol altogether. Although, in the first instance, the worker hopes that the client/patient will speak openly and focus on what is bothering them, different types of questions may be used to gain further information about a specific issue, to encourage fuller responses, or to direct or structure a conversation.

> Many reluctant clients may need only to find genuineness, reassurance, and the right invitation from a counsellor [worker] to begin a relationship. When working with such clients, it is essential to allow them time to feel comfortable and develop trust, to refrain from pre-judging clients' moods, motives and needs, and to try out more than the normal variety of invitiations to talk or participate.
>
> (Munro, Manthei and Small 1983:46)

Open invitations are useful to get the client/patient started and might include:

'How can I help you?'

'Tell me how you feel.'

'What is it that is bothering you?'

If the response is hesitant at first, observe the client's/patient's non-verbal communications, provide some feedback, and repeat the open invitation.

'You seem very tense. Would you like to tell me what is bothering you?'

'You look rather unhappy. Is that how you feel?'

'Something is bothering you. How can I help you?'

Even the most reticent clients/patients will find it difficult not to engage in conversation when open questions and invitations are used repeatedly. Closed questions that require short, factual answers can be used to gain more information about specific issues or to clarify uncertainties. They can also be used to suggest links to a client/patient between drinking and the related consequences that can be more fully explored at a later stage in the working relationship. For example:

'Do you think your drinking could be causing these headaches and stomach upsets?'

'If you drank a bit less, do you think you would manage to get in to work on time more often?'

'Would you have got into the fight if you hadn't been drinking?'

It is important not to weight such questions so that the client/patient feels forced to respond in a certain way. The questions (and possible responses) would be very different if worded as follows:

'Surely you can see that your drinking is causing these headaches and stomach upsets?'

'You know, don't you, that if you drank less you would get in to work on time?'

'I don't think you would have got into that fight if you hadn't been drinking. Don't you agree?'

Multiple questions may also be confusing for a client/patient and the worker should try to ask only one question at a time. Questions such as:

'When did your drinking become a problem and what effects has it had?'

should be avoided, as the client/patient is virtually being asked to provide information on two things at once. Using a mixture of open and closed questions and active listening will help the worker build a relationship with the client/patient, find out where the difficulties lie and assess the role of alcohol in his life. Before moving to the next stage of helping the client/patient to make changes, it is useful to provide a brief summary of what has been established, highlighting positive aspects as well as negative ones so that the client/patient is not left feeling like a 'problem case'. Good self-esteem is essential if the client/patient is to progress, try out new (possibly risky) behaviour and make changes. Low self-esteem could lead to the worker being rejected — 'I'm in such a hopeless mess that you can't help me' — or could create a self-fulfilling prophecy.

Increasing self-esteem

If a drinker has low self-esteem and tends not to value himself, it is unlikely that he will feel motivated to make changes and may reject or block any type of intervention from the professional worker. At this point, the worker should make every effort to help clients/patients increase their self-esteem so that they feel better about themselves and about their relationships and more optimistic about the possibility of change and improvement. Most people prefer praise to criticism but showering praise on clients or patients will not affect their level of self-esteem unless they respect and trust the person who is praising them and can accept what is being said for themselves. The latter part of this chapter includes a practical exercise on increasing self-esteem but in general, workers' comments should related to clients'/patients' strengths, qualities and good points which are:

1. Based on fact and not simply imagined or hoped for by the workers.
2. Reasonably immediate. A client/patient is unlikely to feel reassured if told 'you used to be much happier/fitter/more in control when you were younger.'
3. Accepted by the client/patient.
4. Repeated by the client/patient. The simple act of saying something good and positive about oneself out loud can be a powerful reinforcer.

If working in a family context, the worker might also seek to involve family members in increasing the drinker's self-esteem. This is important as our self-esteem increases or diminishes according to how we *think* we perform within given contexts and the feedback on our behaviour given to us by others.

> Many of the beliefs, attitudes, and behaviours we exhibit have been largely determined by the relevant groups in our life. Our family, friends, classmates, and work associates are only a few of the groups whose norms shape our own.
>
> (Zimbardo, Ebbeson and Maslach 1977:42)

While working as an alcohol and drug counsellor, I was asked to see an elderly lady who wanted some advice about her husband's behaviour. She had chosen to come to an alcohol agency as her husband, once a coal miner and heavy drinker, still drank every day and she thought that his alcohol consumption might be linked to his odd behaviour. He was constantly picking arguments with her about the fact that household items were not returned to their 'proper place' after use and had begun to accuse her of being 'mad'. She was extremely upset and, when unable to offer explanations for the iron being found in the oven or teacups being found in the fridge, began to think she was, indeed, mad. Her self-esteem was very low in view of the constant abuse she received from her husband and she actually asked me to tell her whether I thought she was mad or not. After hearing about her husband's history of heavy drinking and that, although in his late seventies, his daily consumption included at least five pints of beer, I suspected him of being fuddled and confused rather than his wife. With her assistance, we devised a simple system of noting down which household items she used and where she returned them and, in a short time, it became clear that it was her husband who was misplacing the items. Although unable to do anything about her husband's drinking beyond exploring ways for her to cope with it, at least the elderly lady left with her self-esteem restored and no longer fearing she was mad. Thus, the feedback we receive from other people can be influential in increasing or decreasing our self-esteem.

Giving and receiving feedback

During the course of a working relationship with a client or patient, the worker will need to provide feedback on progress or lack of it, and will need to elicit feedback from the client/patient to assess feelings, attitudes, and perceptions and to ensure mutual understanding. Feedback is an important part of alcohol education as it provides an opportunity to emphasize and appreciate changes made by the client/patient in terms of attitudes or behaviour. If the worker and client/patient have set goals between them and have found that they have not been achieved, feedback can be used to highlight this and to restate the position before going on to consider why progress has not been made and how obstacles or difficulties can be overcome. Also, if teaching a client/patient new skills in resisting the pressure to accept drinks from friends or in restructuring what was originally 'drinking time', the worker should elicit feedback to ensure that the client/patient has fully understood what has been said and feels comfortable about using the skills taught.

To help the client/patient, effective feedback should be given in a supportive and constructive manner. On some occasions, it may be necessary to give negative as well as positive feedback and there are ways of doing this so that the process feels comfortable for both the worker and the client/patient. Health and welfare professionals may feel uncomfortable about giving negative feedback on behaviour, but ignoring it means that an unsatisfactory situation is likely to continue and that changes will not be made. Turner (1983) in his book *Developing Interpersonal Skills* (Chapter 5), advocates a four-stage process that allows a worker to give the client/patient negative feedback and to challenge behaviour, while remaining supportive and non-aggressive (see Table 7.2).

Table 7.2 Four-stage process for challenging behaviour

1. Make an objective statement about the behaviour:
   'Last week you didn't reduce your drinking at all.'

2. Describe the effect of this on you:
   'This makes me feel that you haven't used the strategies we discussed.'

3. Make a request for a change:
   'I'd like to go back and discuss them again.'

4. Invite the client or patient to comment:
   'How do you feel about doing that?'

In this way it is the *behaviour* that is challenged and not the client himself. The position is stated, the worker gives feedback and challenges in a non-threatening manner, and the client is given a chance to respond. The worker does not pass judgement but, rather, describes a specific situation, proposes a course of action and invites the client to comment on his reaction and feelings. If possible, the worker should aim to sandwich negative feedback between positive feedback and check that the client has heard both. Also, it is important to challenge behaviour that a client can actually do something about.

Positive	'You have done really well to fill in your drinker's diary for last week.'
Negative	'You haven't managed to reduce your consumption though.'
Positive	'I think you had a good grasp of the strategies we discussed to cut down your drinking.'
Client can act	'Shall we have another look at them to see which ones you can use next week?'

Changing behaviour

If changes in behaviour are to be made, both the worker and client/patient should acknowledge that the process may be a slow one and may need to be built, at first, on seemingly small changes and achievements. It is encouraging to note however, that a reduction in alcohol consumption can lead to speedy results in terms of weight loss, a less bloated or puffy appearance, an improved appetite and digestion, and the ability to sleep. The drinker may also feel more in control of his life and may be willing to make further changes to his life style and drinking behaviour.

In discussing possible changes in behaviour, the worker and client/patient should look at the types of behaviour in which there is a weak investment and aim to change those first, before tackling more treasured habits. In this way, each achievement can be built on so that the client both sees and *feels* the progress he is making. The worker can facilitate this process by providing support, giving positive and negative feedback, and showing that support will continue, even if the hoped-for progress is not made. (See Chapter 9 on education for relapse situations.)

Translating plans into action

If the client or patient is to take action that may lead to behaviour change, he needs to understand why he is doing it, what the possible effects and outcomes are likely to be and what advantages or disadvantages there may be for him and others around him. The worker's role is to help the client/patient understand what changes could be made, help him to develop the skills needed to implement the changes and to support him throughout the period of change. As Egan (1986) says, 'the function of the helper is to get clients to apply problem solving to their current problem situations and to increase the probability that clients will take problem-solving approaches to future problems in living' p. 26.

Strategies are means of achieving goals and, having jointly agreed some goals, the worker and client need to be aware of the range of strategies for achieving these goals. Details of different strategies and their purpose are given in the latter part of this chapter, with a selection of practical exercises to support them. One of the first tasks of the worker, however, may be to educate the client/patient and provide him with some factual information on alcohol and its effects. As we saw in Chapter 3, people receive very little formal education about alcohol and learn about it partly through their own experience and partly from information they receive from peers, colleagues, and family members. The information gleaned is in turn, shaped and influenced by the cultural context, social norms, and the portrayal of alcohol in the media. It is easy to understand how such an array of influences and sources of information give rise to factual misunderstandings and fallacies about alcohol, its effects, and its role in society. Providing clear, accurate, factual information will enable a client/patient to distinguish fact from fiction and will provide a sound base of understanding from which to explore values, attitudes, and behaviour. The following list details factual areas related to alcohol that should be clearly understood by anyone who drinks and not just those whose drinking causes them problems:

1. Units of alcohol and guidelines for healthy, harm-free drinking.

2. Absorption and metabolization.

3. Alcohol and calories.

4. Effects of alcohol and blood-alcohol levels.

5. Drinking and driving.

6. Women and alcohol.

The following section gives factual information about each of these areas and is used to provide the basis for the series of practical exercises in alcohol education given at the end of this chapter.

Units of alcohol

If workers are to help and encourage their clients/patients to assess how much they are drinking and, possibly, monitor their consumption over a period of time, they need a simple system with which to tot up alcohol consumption whether clients/patients drink spirits, beers, or wines, or even a mixture of all three. An easy way to do this is to convert all types of alcoholic drinks into standard units of alcohol, so that clients/patients can understand how many units of alcohol they drink in a day or a week and can compare their consumption levels with guidelines for healthy, harm-free drinking. Figure 7.1 shows different types of alcoholic drinks represented as standard units of alcohol, while Table 7.3 gives the number of units of alcohol contained in many different types of beverage. The important thing to work out is how many units of alcohol a person drinks, whether he is a wine drinker or a lager drinker. It should be remembered that this information relates to standard pub measures of beer, wine, sherry, or spirits and that, at home, we are quite likely to be more generous when pouring a glass of wine or whisky! Encourage clients/ patients to consider what types of alcoholic drinks they consume most often and to become familiar with the process of working out their consumption in terms of units of alcohol.

Table 7.3 How many units of alcohol do you drink?

Beers and lagers		Units
Ordinary strength beer	½ pint	1
or lager	1 pint	2
	1 can	1½
Export beer	1 pint	2½
	1 can	2
Strong ale or lager	½ pint	2
	1 pint	4
	1 can	3
CIDERS		
Average cider	½ pint	1½
	1 pint	3
	quart bottle	6
Strong cider	½ pint	2
	1 pint	4
	quart bottle	8
SPIRITS		
	1 standard single measure	1
	1 standard single measure (¼ gill)	1½
	1/5 gill measure	1¼
	1/3 gill measure	2
	1 bottle	30
TABLE WINE		
(including cider wine	1 standard glass	1
and barley wine)	1 bottle	7
	1 litre bottle	10
SHERRY AND FORTIFIED WINE		
	1 standard small measure	1
	1 bottle	12

These figures are approximate

Source: Health Education Council (1986).

Figure 7.1 Units of alcohol

HOW MUCH ALCOHOL?

EQUIVALENT MEASURES (UNITS)

½ pt beer 1 glass table wine 1 glass sherry 1 single whisky unit alcohol

THE AMOUNT OF ALCOHOL THAT THE LIVER CAN BREAKDOWN IN 1 HOUR = 1 UNIT

Source: Sinnett, Wright, and Evans (1983).

It is difficult to provide hard-and-fast rules about levels of alcohol consumption for healthy, harm-free drinking as there are several mitigating factors that should be taken into account. These include sex, body weight, age, tolerance of alcohol, and frequency of consumption. These factors will be explored in more detail further on but the following limits for drinking are suggested as guidelines for weekly consumption:

	Men	*Women*
Cut down if you are drinking	More than 35 units	More than 20 units
Consider cutting down if you drink	21-34 units	14-19 units
Keep to	Up to 20 units	Up to 14 units

If clients and patients find that their weekly levels of consumption consistently fall into the higher categories, they significantly increase the risk of causing physical damage to themselves and/or becoming physically dependent on alcohol.

Frequency of consumption is also an important factor and it is better to spread drinking over several days, rather than to consume a lot of units on only one or two occasions. Even though a man drinks less than 20 units in a week, he may increase his chances of having an accident or getting into a fight if he drinks them all on one occasion. Also, it is better not to drink every day and to drink 'four to six units two or three times per week (men) or three to four units two or three times per week (women). This gives your body the chance to recover from the effects of alcohol in between drinking sessions' (Robertson and Heather 1986:19).

Absorption and metabolization of alcohol

There are a lot of misunderstandings about how alcohol gets into the blood stream, what it does while it is there, and how it leaves the body. When a person drinks, the alcohol goes down into the stomach where approximately one-fifth of it is absorbed directly into the bloodstream. If there is food in the stomach, the alcohol will be absorbed more slowly and the person will not get intoxicated so quickly. Alternatively, if the stomach is empty, both absorption and intoxication will be more rapid.

Other factors that affect the absorption rate of alcohol include:

1. *A high concentration of alcohol.* For example, spirits are absorbed more quickly than drinks with a low concentration such as beers or lagers.
2. *Sugar.* The sugars in sweet drinks tend to retard the rate of absorption.
3. *Fizzy drinks.* The gas in fizzy drinks such as champagne or sparkling wines increases the rate of absorption. This is also true for mixers such as tonic, lemonade, or ginger ale.

The remainder of the alcohol passes through the stomach into the small intestine and is absorbed into the bloodstream.

Once in the bloodstream, alcohol circulates rapidly round the body affecting every organ, including the brain (see Chapter 3). Some people imagine that they eliminate alcohol from their bodies by going to the toilet or 'sweating it off'. In reality, the body can only eliminate 2–5 per cent of alcohol unchanged through the kidneys (urine), the lungs (breath), and in sweat. The rest of the alcohol has to be broken down by the liver.

The liver is like a car with only one gear — it can only work at one rate. The liver can only burn up one standard drink [unit] in an hour. If it has to deal with too much alcohol over a number of years, it suffers damage.

(Health Education Council, 1986:9)

Alcohol and calories

In the liver, alcohol is turned into a source of energy that can be used by the body. If the energy is not used it will be stored as fat and, since alcohol contains a lot of calories, heavy drinkers may find that they have problems with their weight. Even the low-sugar diet beers can contribute to weight problems. They may contain less sugar than ordinary beers but they also contain more alcohol, and alcohol itself is rich in calories.

Paradoxically, heavy drinking may make someone fat but it may also cause them to suffer from malnutrition. If food is replaced with alcoholic drinks, the body will not receive sufficient essential nutrients and vitamins. Excessive alcohol consumption impairs the body's ability to absorb vitamins and may lead to vitamin deficiency. If a person eats normally but drinks to excess as well, he is likely to put on weight because the additional intake of calories cannot be burned up and must be stored as fat. Table 7.4 gives a guide to the calorific values of different types of drinks. Encourage clients/patients to be aware of the calorie intake from their alcohol consumption and explore ways of reducing it if it is perceived as a problem.

Table 7.4 Calorie value of alcoholic drinks

Measure	Drink	Calories
½ pint	Beer	80–125
	Cider	90–180
	Lager	100–120
	Stout	95–210
Single pub measure 1/6 gill	Brandy	55
	Gin	55
	Whisky	55
Single pub measure 1/3 gill	Sweet sherry	70–140
	Dry sherry	60–80
	Port	80–165
Small glass	Dry wine	75–80
	Sweet wine	80–110

Source: Simnett, Wright, and Evans (1983).

Effects of alcohol and blood-alcohol levels

In Chapter 3 we considered some of the short- and long-term effects of alcohol on both the body (physical effects) and on behaviour (psychological effects). The degree to which a drinker is affected — either physically or psychologically — depends on the concentration of alcohol in the bloodstream. This is often referred to as the blood-alcohol level or BAL and is used by the police, for example, to assess whether an intoxicated person is legally fit to drive (see section on drinking and driving p. 105–6.) The BAL gives a measure of how intoxicated a person is and is usually expressed in milligrams of alcohol per 100 millilitres of blood. Although it is not necessary to get too technical, clients/patients may find that they regularly experience certain difficulties when their blood-alcohol levels are high. These may include frequently getting into arguments or fights, experiencing blackouts, loss of memory, or having accidents.

If they are to change their behaviour, they need to recognize the levels of drinking that cause or contribute to these situations. In general, one unit of alcohol will raise a man's BAL to 15 milligrams per 100 millilitres of blood and a woman's to 20 milligrams. The body needs approximately one hour to get rid of one unit of alcohol and Figure 7.2 shows how long it takes for the effects of alcohol to wear off.

Figure 7.2 How quickly do the effects wear off?

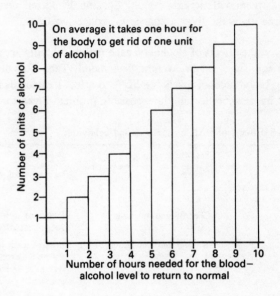

A person's BAL, however, may also be affected by the following factors:

1. *Height*. One unit of alcohol will have a greater effect on a small person than a large person. The small person has a smaller volume of blood, and, therefore, a higher blood-alcohol level.

2. *Fat*. One unit of alcohol will have a greater effect on a fat person than on a lean, muscular person of the same weight. Fatty tissue has a poor blood supply and, in a fat person, the blood-alcohol level will be more concentrated.

3. *Water*. The less water a person has in their body, the more concentrated the alcohol will be. Women have less water in their bodies than men and are likely to have a higher proportion of fat. Women are also smaller than men on the whole and will experience higher concentrations of alcohol in their blood than men who drink the same amount of alcohol.

4. *Speed of consumption*. If a person drinks alcohol more quickly than the liver can break it down, the concentration of alcohol in the bloodstream will increase rapidly. Spacing drinks out over a period of time gives the liver a chance to reduce the BAL.

Obviously, the effects of alcohol on each individual will vary according to their sex, age, height, weight, and mood. Table 7.5 details how differing blood-alcohol levels are *likely* to affect individuals and could be used by workers to highlight possible problem areas for clients.

Table 7.5 Effects of BAL on feelings and behaviour

BAL	Feelings	Behaviour
40 mg (per 100ml of blood	Relaxed	Increased risk of accidents
60 mg	Cheerful and outgoing	Reactions slowed down Judgement affected
80 mg	Warmth and well-being	Loss of some inhibitions and self-control. Slowed reactions. Driving impaired.
120 mg	Emotional, excitable	Talkative Acts on impulse. Mood swings May be withdrawn
150 mg	Confused	Slurred speech. Possibly aggressive
200 mg	Drunk	Staggering. Double vision. Hearing affected. Memory loss
300 mg		Unconsciousness possible
400 mg		Unconsciousness likely. Death not unknown
500 mg		Death possible
600 mg		Death probable

Drinking and driving

The legal limits for drinking and driving vary from country to country. When the concept of testing drivers' blood-alcohol levels was first introduced, some countries set fairly high legal levels initially. For example, in Sweden the original legal limit was set at 150mg per 100ml of blood, although it has since been lowered to 50mg. As the numbers of alcohol-related road accidents have continued to increase however, and research has provided more information on the effects of alcohol on people's ability to drive safely, many countries have lowered their limits considerably. In Victoria and Western Australia today, the limit is 50mg although drivers in the rest of Australia are permitted to drive with up to 80mg of alcohol in their blood. In the fifty states of the USA the limit ranges from 50–100mg with severe penalties for those caught driving over those limits. In the USSR, Bulgaria, East Germany, and Poland the limit is 20mg and some countries — Czechoslovakia, Saudi Arabia, and Turkey — do not permit drinking and driving at all and have a zero limit. Attitudes to the drinking driver have started to change however, as Denney points out:

> there is a general trend to lower legal drink-drive limits, more
> positive law enforcement and attempts at special guidance for
> second and third offenders in some countries. At the same time
> drinking and driving is being treated as a more serious offence
> than it was twenty or thirty years ago.

(Denney 1986:63)

Whatever the limit, we know that alcohol affects our ability to drive — to see clearly, to judge distances and speeds accurately, and to react quickly — and that, the more we drink, the more we are affected. In Great Britain, the greatest cause of death in young men is road accidents that occur after drinking and more than half of all people breathalysed by the police are found to have a blood-alcohol level of more than twice the legal limit. Even with a legal limit for drinking and driving set at 80mg of alcohol per 100ml of blood, we know that our chances of having an accident increase four times if we drink up to this level.

In addition, because each individual is different and will be affected by the factors given in the preceding section, it is virtually impossible to set levels of drinking that are universally safe when it comes to driving. It is best to follow a policy of not drinking at all when driving, rather than attempting to drink up to certain limits, even though they may be legal. It is often forgotten that, as the body can only get rid of one unit of alcohol per hour, it is possible to indulge in a heavy drinking session one evening and *still* be over the legal limit for driving the following morning. Alternatively, someone who has several units of alcohol at lunchtime and 'tops up' with another two or three on the way home in the evening may find that he is over the legal limit. People who drink and drive regularly may not be concerned about such facts and often put forward the following justifications for continuing:

'I always drive more carefully when I've had a few drinks'.

'If I've been drinking I'm always careful to keep to the speed limits and watch the traffic lights.'

'I've been doing it for so long that the car knows its own way home by now.'

Whatever the argument or justification put forward, the fact is that alcohol impairs our ability to drive safely. It only takes one emergency situation requiring quick reactions or a momentary loss of attention at the wheel to result in an accident involving injury or death. Workers should encourage clients/patients to acknowledge that, the longer they continue to drink and drive, the more they increase their chances of being stopped by the police and/or causing an accident.

Women and alcohol

Because of the differences in height, weight, and their fat and body water ratio, women experience the effects of alcohol more quickly than men and are more likely to suffer physical damage at an earlier stage than men. There are also other alcohol-related issues that women drinkers should be aware of, including alcohol and the menstrual cycle, alcohol and pregnancy, alcohol and contraceptives, and alcohol and other drugs.

A woman's reaction to alcohol is likely to vary during her menstrual cycle. In the premenstrual phase or while ovulating, many women find that they are more suseptible to alcohol and feel its effects more quickly. In her book *Women under the Influence*, Brigid McConville (1983) says, 'It could be that alcohol is absorbed more fully and quickly and with increased effect when women are premenstrual. Our tissues at this time are more ready to retain water and so may retain more alcohol in that water' (p. 84). Women experiencing premenstrual tension may use alcohol deliberately to relieve feelings of anxiety, irritability, or depression and, although this is not necessarily problematic, they should be wary of relying on alcohol in this way.

In general, although women are affected more quickly by alcohol than men — especially during the premenstrual phase or ovulation — they also metabolize it more quickly. Women who take the contraceptive pill, however, have a more regular response to alcohol 'throughout' the menstrual cycle but will metabolize alcohol more slowly and stay drunk longer. Professionals working with women clients or patients should encourage them to be aware of their menstrual cycle and how it affects their levels of consumption and responses to alcohol.

Drinking alcohol during pregnancy can damage the foetus and may result in babies being born with a wide range of physical and/or mental defects. This range of defects is known collectively as foetal alcohol syndrome or FAS and is not a risk only for those women who drink very heavily.

> There is a lot of research to show that even moderate drinking during pregnancy — just a few drinks a day — *can* have harmful effects on the foetus. Of course, these harmful effects do not always occur — once again, it is a matter of risks — but when they do occur, they seem to be a less pronounced version of FAS, including poor birth weight and lowered IQ.
>
> (Robertson and Heather 1986:64–5)

No-one knows exactly how FAS is caused or in what quantities and on which occasions alcohol will affect the foetus. Some researchers have found that even low levels of alcohol consumption (two drinks per day) can almost double the chances that a baby will be stillborn, will be smaller than normal, or will suffer from some other congenital effect (Streissguth 1979). A further theory is that the first three months are critical in a pregnancy and that regular, excessive consumption and/or bouts of drunkenness should be avoided during this period.

> Another theory is that there could be a particular critical period during pregnancy when the foetus is especially vulnerable to damage from alcohol. This might explain why babies with FAS features have been born to mothers who had just a few drinks now and then, as well as to women who drank rarely but heavily.
>
> (McConville 1983:99)

107

Women are best advised to cut out alcohol completely when pregnant or planning to become pregnant or, if they must drink, to keep to one or two units only on each occasion. They should also avoid bouts of drunkenness at any stage in the pregnancy. Of course, it may be several weeks before a woman actually realizes she is pregnant and, if she has continued to drink, she may be anxious about having damaged the foetus already. The worker should explain that this is not a foregone conclusion — it is a question of increasing or decreasing risks. After birth, nursing mothers should also be made aware of the way in which alcohol will be passed to the baby through breast milk. In addition, alcohol may impair a mother's ability to breast feed her child and may make feeding more difficult (Dowdell 1981). Women experiencing difficulties with breast feeding should ignore advice to have one or two drinks to help them relax.

Although men are also involved in procreation, there is little research available on the effects of heavy drinking on a man's ability to create a healthy foetus. Brigid McConville states that 'Drink is a testicular toxin and heavy drinking in men (five or more drinks a day) can result in reduced production of sperm and production of abnormal sperm' (McConville 1983:96). It is not known whether this affects the foetus at the time of conception.

Finally, women are more likely than men to use psychotropic (mood-altering) drugs and, because alcohol is also a psychotropic drug, should be wary about mixing them. Alcohol has a depressant effect on the central nervous system and, combined with other depressant drugs, will multiply (potentiate) its effects. In other instances, alcohol will reduce the effects of some drugs such as antibiotics and anticoagulants so that their therapeutic benefits are decreased. The following is a list of common types of drugs that do not react well with alcohol:

Type of drug	Effects when taken with alcohol
Barbiturates, sleeping pills, hypnotics	Dangerous, possible lethal combination. Effect of alcohol and drug is multiplied several times.
Antihistamines	Greatly increased drowsiness
Antidepressants	Slowed co-ordination and greatly reduced concentration
Antibiotics, anticoagulants	Reduced therapeutic effect

Analgesics, aspirin   Increased risk of stomach irritation, stomach
                             bleeding. Difficulty in blood clotting

It is best not to mix alcohol with any other type of drug. If a client/
patient drinks regularly and/or excessively and is also taking medication, workers should alert him or her to the possibility of a bad reaction
and should seek the prescribing doctor's advice.

Alcohol education exercises

The following section contains some practical exercises in alcohol education for use with clients or patients. Workers should ensure that the client/
patient has a sound knowledge base (units of alcohol, blood-alcohol levels,
metabolization, etc.) before attempting to use the exercises. Each exercise
has a purpose, detailing its aims and what it is intended to achieve, a
materials/preparation section describing which materials are needed and
what should be prepared in advance, and a method section describing how
to use the exercise. The exact timing of each exercise is left to the worker to
decide, as flexibility is desirable when working with individuals. The exercises are not set out in any particular order and are not intended to be used as
a developmental sequence. Rather than go through each one in order,
workers should decide on which areas of their clients'/patients' drinking
they wish to concentrate (monitoring or controlling consumption, increasing
self-awareness, changing behaviour) and choose an appropriate exercise.

Monitoring exercises

Drinker's diary

Purpose To help individuals monitor their daily/weekly alcohol
consumption. To highlight patterns of drinking behaviour.

Materials/preparation Copy of the drinker's diary (Table 7.6) Ensure
the individual understands the concept of units of alcohol.

Method Explain that this is a useful way of monitoring drinking
behaviour and that if a diary is kept over a period of weeks, it may
highlight certain patterns of behaviour i.e. drinking in response to stress
or depression. Recap on the concept of counting drinks in terms of units
of alcohol and ask the individual to fill in the diary each day. Explain

Table 7.6 Drinker's Diary

	When?	Where?	Who With?	Why/What Mood?	What?	How Much?	With Food?	Units
Monday								
Tuesday								
Wednesday								
Thursday								
Friday								
Saturday								
Sunday								

that cheating and minimizing the amount drunk will help no-one, least of all the drinker! Before completion, check that the client is filling it in as you have explained.

Once the diary has been completed, discuss it with the client/patient. Are there any particular 'heavy-drinking' days? If so, what caused them? Do certain situations (drinking alone or in the company of particular friends) lead to increased consumption? Does the weekly total exceed the levels for safe drinking? Where and how can reductions be made?

Calorie-counting diary

Purpose To help individuals monitor their calorie intake through drinking.

Materials/preparation Copy of the calorie-counting diary (Table 7.7). Ensure that the individual has a good knowledge of the calorific values of different drinks. (See section on alcohol and calories p. 102).

Method Ask the individual to complete the calorie-counting diary for a week and, once completed, discuss the results. If the calorie intake is excessive and is causing or contributing to a weight problem, discuss

Table 7.7 Calorie-counting diary

	Drinks	*Calories*
Monday		
Tuesday		
Wednesday		
Thursday		
Friday		
Saturday		
Sunday		
	WEEKLY TOTAL	

how and where reductions could be made. Could alternative drinks be substituted with low-calorie mixers or could the individual resolve not to drink on certain days?

Controlling/reducing consumption

Refusing drinks

Purpose To help the individual feel confident enough to refuse drinks or order non-alcoholic alternatives.

Materials/preparation Brainstorm with the individual all possible ways of refusing a drink or of ordering a non-alcoholic drink.

Method Working with the individual, encourage him to select three or four feasible ways of refusing a drink from the brainstorm list. Use role play to allow him to practise refusing or ordering a non-alcoholic drink. If the individual finds it difficult to refuse a drink in the company of one particular friend or a group of friends, ask him to act the part of the friend(s) while you, the worker, use suggestions from the brainstorm list to resist the pressure to drink alcohol. Discuss the feelings and the difficulties encountered.

Setting limits

Purpose To help the individual set appropriate limits for drinking. To explore ways of achieving this.

Materials/preparation It will be helpful if the individual has kept a drinker's diary over a period of weeks and has discussed with the worker where and how to cut down on consumption.

Method Consider the individual's total weekly alcohol consumption and assess how far it exceeds the recommended levels for safe, harm-free drinking. Working with the individual, discuss how and where reduction in consumption could be made. Could the drinker resolve to reduce consumption by two/three/four units on each drinking occasion or could he decide to have one/two/three alcohol-free days each week?

Once a decision to cut down on drinking has been made, brainstorm

112

all possible ways to achieve this. Such a brainstorm might include some of the following:

start drinking later	have soft drinks now and again
drink more slowly	eat before/while drinking
avoid round-buying	take days off from drinking

Encourage the individual to select and practise some of these points and discuss the results.

Self-awareness

Road map

Purpose To encourage individuals to see drinking behaviour in terms of a continuum. To explore good/bad life experiences and relate these to good/bad drinking experiences.

Materials/preparation Paper and pen

Method Encourage the individual to draw his life as a road that starts at birth and finishes in the present and incorporates all the major twists and turns and ups and down that he has experienced to date. Explain that it is important to include good aspects as well as bad ones and ask the individual to highlight major life events such as childhood, education, adolescence, relationships/friendships, jobs, marriage, children, accidents, illness, etc.

When the road map has been drawn, encourage the individual to identify his attitudes to drinking and drinking behaviour at each stage and add these to the map. If the individual is willing, discuss the major life events that have been highlighted and examine the role that has been played by alcohol.

Balance sheet

Purpose To encourage the individual to weigh up the advantages and disadvantages of different types of drinking behaviour.

Materials/preparation Copy of the balance sheet (Table 7.8).

Method Explain the purpose of the exercise and decide with the individual which type or types of drinking behaviour will be considered. These might include looking at the pros and cons of:

drinking in the morning/at lunchtime

drinking alone

drinking at work

weekend drinking

drinking spirits/beers/wines

drunkenness

drinking over certain limits (define these in advance)

Whichever type of drinking behaviour is chosen, encourage the individual to fill in the balance sheet highlighting the positive and negative spin-offs from drinking. Discuss ways in which the individual can maximize the positive spin-offs or achieve them in different ways and minimize the negative ones.

Table 7.8 Balance sheet of drinking

	Positive spin-offs	*Negative spin-offs*
Feelings (physical and mental)		
Relationships and friendships		
Finances		
Work		
Others		

Troublesome/trouble-free drinking

Purpose To increase awareness of circumstances that contribute to troublesome or trouble-free drinking occasions.

Materials/preparation Copy of the troublesome/trouble-free drinking occasions sheet (Table 7.9).

Method Explain how the sheet is to be filled in and encourage the drinker to complete it:

1. on a day-to-day basis if he is drinking regularly, or
2. each time he has a drinking occasion.

Discuss the results together and look for circumstances that contribute to troublesome drinking occasions. Does the amount of alcohol consumed play a part? Is troublesome drinking linked to particular bars or pubs or with particular friends and drinking companions? Does the amount of time spent drinking seem significant?

Look at the drinking occasions that have been trouble-free. What makes them different? Discuss the factors involved and consider which personal rules the individual could set himself to avoid or eliminate some of the more risky circumstances.

Table 7.9 (a) Troublesome drinking occasions

Day	Time	Hours spent	Where?	With whom?	Other activities?	Units	Money spent	Any consequences?
Fri	5.30 – 10.30 pm	5	Pub crawl in town	Steve, Simon, and John	None	12	£8	Missed bus home Hangover next day
Sat	7.00 – 1.00 am	6	Local bar and party at Simon's	Brian, Simon Steve, and Ian	None	15	£10	Was sick Argument with taxi driver
Thurs	6.30 – 10.30 pm	4	Local pub	John and Simon	Watched snooker game	13	£7	Bad night's sleep Headache Late for work

(b) Troublefree drinking occasions

Day	Time	Hours spent	Where?	With whom?	Other activities	Units	Money spent	Any consequences?
Tues	8.00 – 10.00 pm	2	Indian Restaurant	Wife Alison and another couple	Eating	6	£5	
Sat	9.00 – 12.00 pm	3	Local club	Brian, Ian, and Phil	Playing cards	8	£4	
Fri	8.00 – 10.30 pm	2½	Local bar	Phil and Frank	Quiz game	7	£3.50	Won the quiz!

Working with the family

When working with an individual who is experiencing problems related to drinking, it is important to remember that he may also have a family whose members are affected by the drinking behaviour or, at least, a support network of peers, relatives, or colleagues who have become concerned or involved. Such people may not only be affected by the individual's drinking but may also, wittingly or otherwise, trigger it, encourage it, or allow it to continue. In families where alcohol has become a problem, there may also be feelings of confusion, guilt, shame, and anger that need to be confronted and explored if progress is to be made and more constructive family functioning is to be encouraged.

> The stress of accomodating the problem drinker in the family may present in various ways: sometimes the children will present behaviour disorders which reveal underlying family difficulties, sometimes the spouse actively asks for help, or experiences his or her own pathological reaction to the strains imposed by living with a person with an alcohol problem, sometimes the entire family system breaks down or its functions become so impaired so as to require professional help and intervention.
>
> (Lawrence and Cran 1987:63)

Even if the individual denies the problem and is unwilling to co-operate, workers may find that other family members or members of the support system will benefit from alcohol education designed to help them better understand and cope with the problem situation.

In his paper 'Alcohol problems and the family' (1987, p. 76–81), Orford highlights two influential models for use with families where drinking is a problem. The first, known as the stress-victim model, supposes that the individual's drinking has a stressful impact on other family members who search for and practise different ways of coping with the stress. The non-excessively drinking members of the family need help, partly because they themselves are at risk due to the stress they are under and partly because the coping strategies they develop and use will, in turn, affect the future course of the drinking problem. The impact of alcohol problems can be wide and varied and the stress generated may be short-, mid-, or long-term. Whatever the circumstances, alcohol education can help family members gain a clearer understanding of the problem and may assist them in assessing and possibly improving their coping behaviour.

The second model, a family-systems perspective, sees the family as a system in which individuals are not picked out as the 'stress-victim' or the 'problem drinker'.

> The alcoholic individual becomes the 'alcoholic family'. In this process the symptomatic member of the family is termed the 'identified patient' — i.e. the alcoholic member becomes the member identified to represent for the whole family a particular piece of disturbance.
>
> (Steinglass: 1982).

Each individual has an interdependent role to play within the system and excessive drinking is seen as purposive, adaptive, and meaningful to the family as a whole and not just to the drinker. Using this perspective, workers would try to assess what functions excessive drinking serves for the whole family and might consider whether excessive drinking on the part of one family member was a sign of a problem or a dysfunction among other family members. From this perspective, alcohol education could help the whole family to understand its patterns of behaviour and how its individual members interrelate and could provide strategies to help the family undergo and accept change. Orford comments:

> The danger is probably in adhering too rigidly to one or another extreme viewpoint. Systems thinking alone carries the danger of losing sight of the commonsense approach that partners and children are victims of the excessive drinking with which they must learn to cope in the best possible way, whilst stress-victim thinking alone runs the risk of ignoring the interactional nature

of family life and the possible family functions, which continued excessive drinking may be serving.

(Orford, 1987)

If workers are aware of both models, they will probably appreciate that elements of each are common and applicable to work with families where alcohol has become a problem and will seek to improve the physical and emotional well-being and functioning ability of not only the individual but of the family unit as a whole.

Effect on the family

To date, most research has concentrated on families in which the husband/father is the problem drinker and has considered the effects of excessive drinking on the wife and children. Little work has been done on the impact of drinking on men who are married to women problem drinkers.

The effect of problem drinking on families, the degree of hardship they may suffer, their chosen methods of coping, and the possible outcomes are concepts that vary from one family to another. Orford (1987) warns, 'It is important not to make sweeping generalisations about "alcoholic marriages", as it is important not to make unsupported generalisations about all "alcoholics" or problem drinkers' but puts forward two broad, fairly distinct phases in family life associated with a worsening alcohol problem in the husband. In the first stage, the family recognizes the problem and the wife attempts to control the husband's drinking. This may include confrontation, giving ultimatums, withdrawing affection, or disposing of supplies of alcohol kept in the house. The family may experience increased social isolation as it tries to conceal the problem from those seen as 'outsiders' and the wife may be forced to assume some of her husband's family responsibilities to maintain a facade of 'normality'. In the second stage, when it seems that these strategies do not appear to affect the drinker, family members may experience feelings of fear and hopelessness and may well seek outside help with what they see as 'the problem'.

Excessive alcohol consumption can prevent the drinker from fulfilling certain family roles and responsibilities such as those of parent, lover, supportive partner, or provider. When intoxicated, the drinker may be physically and/or emotionally incapable of fulfilling these roles or may use alcohol deliberately as a reason for avoiding them. In response, the wife may threaten, cajole, collude, or cover up for her drinking husband or may even attempt to join him and become drawn into the drinking behaviour.

Problem drinking within a family can also cause or contribute to many different types of stress or hardship for family members. Increasing social isolation is particularly difficult for children to cope with. If ashamed of or embarrassed by a drinking parent, children may resist forming normal friendships with their peers. They feel unable to bring friends home after school or college and risk becoming increasingly withdrawn from peer-group activities. They fear being seen as 'different' from their friends and take inappropriate responsibility to conceal parental drinking. Financial hardship becomes a factor if a major part of disposable family income is used for alcohol and reductions are made to the general standard of living. There may be an increased risk of physical hardship seen either in violence towards family members themselves or in the destruction of household objects and furniture. This in turn may lead to involvement with the police who are called to deal with domestic disputes and to greater marital instability as the wife threatens to leave or actually leaves the marital home (Orford *et al.* 1976:318–39). As alcohol assumes an increasing importance in the drinker's life, the spouse or partner may be subjected to some degree of emotional deprivation and may perceive the drinking as a form of rejection. It may even be used as such by the drinker who becomes increasingly preoccupied with drinking and takes less and less interest and plays a diminishing part in family life and affairs. Under such internal pressures it seems surprising that many marriages survive at all, although workers should also consider the external pressures at work. Obligations to children, lack of independent income, fear of change or public 'failure', legal difficulties, and lack of alternative accommodation are all factors that weigh against marital breakdown.

Effects on children

There are several concerns to be raised when considering the effects of family drinking problems on children. The more immediate concerns focus on children's emotional, physical, social, and financial well-being, although there are other, equally important concerns that are less easily defined such as consistency, security, and predictability. Children react badly to inconsistency from parents, to poor care provision (as they perceive it), and to lack of security. In a study of the quality of parent-child relationships, Glassner and Loughlin (1987) remark 'when relationships with parents are described as good or bad three issues are raised: basic care, consistency of expectations and communication' (p. 199). Children find it hard to cope with parental unpredictability or with unexplained withdrawal. Excessive alcohol consumption can contribute to these by inducing sudden swings of moods and temperament and, for younger children, it may be difficult to understand the differences between and reasons for sober and intoxicated behaviour on the part of a parent. Children may suffer emotional and/or physical neglect if all the family's attention and energies are focused on the drinker, and their own individual contributions to family life may go unacknowledged. This may result in acting-out behaviour, aggression, bed-wetting, truanting, anxiety, withdrawal, and isolation, which, in turn, can increase pressure on the non-excessively drinking parent. Glassner and Loughlin point out that 'physical security and shelter are not taken for granted. They are signs of parental love and concern' and that when children 'feel unloved by or irrelevant to their parents, they express anger and hurt'. Children need predictability. They can cope with a certain degree of flexibility but are poor at tolerating unexplained changes in parental reactions or responses. It increases their sense of isolation from the family and provides an unsatisfactory role model for their own behaviour.

A further concern for children within a family where alcohol is a problem is that of the role model they are given in relation to alcohol and drinking behaviour. If a parent has a drink problem, how are children likely to perceive alcohol and how might they use it themselves in the future? In *Drug Use and Misuse* (1987:77), Orford cautions against generalizations and points out that the children of problem-drinking parents do not form a homogeneous group. Significant variables include the length of exposure to a parental drinking problem and the age at which exposure takes place. Also, the incidence of violence and the degree of hardship suffered as a result of a parent's drinking will vary enormously. More disturbingly however, there is evidence that suggests that children whose parents are excessive drinkers are more likely to develop alcohol problems in adulthood themselves and it would appear that alcohol problems do run in families (Cotton 1979:89–116). Orford (1987) concludes that 'present evidence therefore suggests that children of problem drinkers represent an important high risk group both because of their proneness to problems during childhood and adolescence, and their proneness to problems in later life'.

121

Roles within the family

If the family unit is seen as an operational system, the behaviour of its members will affect the stability of the system and, conversely, the needs of the family system will affect the behaviour of its individual members. The drinker risks becoming the scapegoat for a number of other family problems and the worker should be prepared to understand and work towards a better functioning family system, rather than working with the drinker in isolation. Even less helpful would be an attempt to remove the drinker from the family situation (unless in need of immediate medical or psychiatric treatment) and then allow him to return to that situation without having helped other family members come to terms with changes in their own and the drinker's behaviour.

Eric Berne's (Berne, 1973) theory of transactional analysis provides a useful model for understanding how attitudes and forms of behaviour are adopted and perpetuated within families and highlights the differing roles taken up by individual family members. Simply explained, Berne puts forward four basic life positions — or views of ourselves and others — that are based on how we perceive our own self-worth and identity (see Figure 8.1).

Figure 8.1 Berne's conceptual framework of life positions

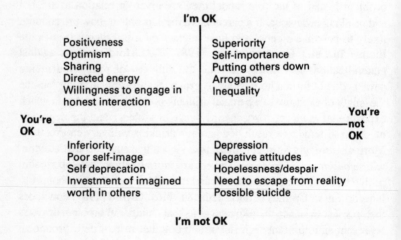

Source: Berne (1973).

In childhood, understanding of self-worth and identity is shaped by information telling us that we either are, or are not 'OK'. If love, approval, and support are freely and consistently given, we feel that we are acceptable, that we have worth in the eyes of others, that we are 'OK'. If, however, love is witheld, given inconsistently, or only under certain conditions, self-esteem tends to be low, we feel unacceptable and see ourselves as not 'OK'. In addition, we take a subjective view of other people around us and put them in a position relative to our own.

As such positions are reinforced throughout childhood, they become familiar and are likely to be repeated in adult life to preserve the status quo with which we feel most comfortable. Within family systems, however, the repetition of such roles often means that openness, honesty, and direct communication are avoided or manipulated to some degree (see Chapter 3, The drinker's family, p. 36–9). Karpman, a close associate of Eric Berne, developed a drama triangle, which provides a helpful model for understanding the roles of different family members and how they may interact and change according to the game being played (Karpman 1969:39). Karpman reduced the four life positions to three basic roles of persecutor, rescuer, and victim (see Figure 8.2), each of which was associated with a particular set of attitudes and responses.

Persecutor
— moralistic, critical, blames others
— self-righteous, full of own importance
— uses punitive methods to enforce unrealistic rules

Rescuer
— offers help, support, and reassurance
— needs to be needed by others
— avoids identifying/acknowledging real issues so that solutions are not found and rescuer role can continue.

Victim
— is helpless, passive, vulnerable
— rationalizes situations by blaming fate, bad luck, or misfortune
— accepts no responsibility for self.

In families, roles will be adopted that create a balanced, functional system that is acceptable to its individual members. The existence of an alcohol problem may disrupt this balance and create dissatisfaction. Members will:

formulate a pattern of behaviour and responses which become an established norm and agreed for the marriage. Changes of behaviour which threaten this equilibrium will be challenged by the assumption of different roles and positions, manipulating the reinstatement of the agreed status quo.

(Lawrence and Cran 1987:65)

Figure 8.2 The Karpman triangle

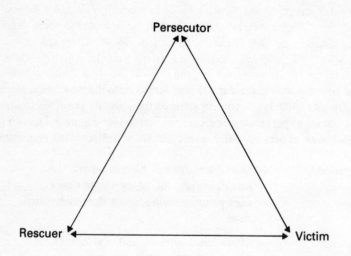

Source: Karpman (1969)

In this situation, players find that previously familiar roles do not bring anticipated attention and approval (strokes) and, if they remain in that role, tend to become increasingly frustrated. They may decide to change roles, to move from the position of persecutor to that of rescuer, but will only gain satisfaction (strokes) if other players change their roles in response. In a study of the wives of problem drinkers in treatment, Albretson and Vaglum observed that:

initially nearly all wives of problem drinkers take on the role of rescuer or dummy. That is, a wife either wants to make life better for a husband with alcohol problems, and take away his need to drink, or deny to herself recognition of the reality of his drinking. Eventually, when these positions no longer work or have any pay-off, the role will be changed to that of persecutor or occasionally bar-tender.

(Albretson and Vaglum 1979)

Workers must avoid being drawn into family games (as explained in Chapter 3) and assuming any of the roles themselves (most typically that of rescuer or persecutor). Instead, they should encourage family members to be aware of their individual roles, how they change and interact and explore ways of diminishing the frequency of game playing and increasing honest, direct communication. The following strategies put forward by Ron Clements may prove helpful for work with family members:

Recognise the games that you most frequently find yourself in and identify those which you initiate and those which you are drawn into.

Learn to recognise the introductory comments which form the invitation into the game, and avoid responding in the expected way. An unexpected response is likely to break up the game.

Stop exaggerating your own weaknesses and other people's strengths. This introduces feelings of 'Not OKness'.

Stop exaggerating your own strengths and other people's weaknesses. This projects attitudes of 'You're not OK'.

Be aware of any tendency to operate as a Persecutor or Rescuer. Either way you will end up as the Victim.

Avoid using negative strokes. Use positive ones instead.

Make conscious efforts to operate from an 'I'm OK — You're OK' position and allow yourself to experience the greater degree of intimacy that this is likely to introduce into the relationship.

(Clements 1980:36)

How families cope

Few families experiencing alcohol problems seek outside help directly and, as a result, are quite likely to have developed various coping

125

strategies within the family system. Two studies that researched how family members coped with drinking problems revealed a range of strategies associated with varying degrees of relative success. (Orford *et al*. 1975:1254–67 and Schaffer and Tyler 1979:431–7.) They include:

pleading	controlling access to drink (pouring it away, making no-drinking rules for the house)
threatening	
rowing	
withdrawing sexually	attacking
avoiding	competing (drinking alongside drinker)
keeping out of the way	taking greater degree of control or responsibility for family matters
being indulgent	
seeking help	taking steps towards separation

The study showed that negative strategies based on avoidance or withdrawal tended to be less successful, relatively speaking, than positive ones that engaged with the drinker at some level and remained involved in attempts to help him. In the latter case, energy and attention was focused on the drinking behaviour rather than the drinker himself.

Other studies have shown similar results and some authors have also paid attention to the coping strategies of children within families where alcohol has become a problem (Meyer 1982 and Seixas 1980). Roles adopted by children within the family are often those of peace maker, counsellor, or avoider in an effort to maintain the homeostasis of the system. Their specific characteristics include:

peace-maker — the child takes on responsibility for other siblings to maintain domestic harmony and the ongoing function of the family system. This may include carrying out age-inappropriate activities such as cooking, shopping, and getting younger children ready for bed at night or for school in the morning.

counsellor — the child is used (inappropriately) as a source of support by either or both parents and is exposed to moral, emotional, or financial dilemmas not appropriate to his age, experience, or understanding.

avoider — the child withdraws physically and/or emotionally from the home environment and shows a strong degree of identification with peers, often those who have violent or problem-drinking parents themselves. Lack of a strong parental role model to provide guidance and support and to confirm identity, may lead the child to find a substitute parent model in a close relative or adult friend.

Among the few studies of the impact of a mother's/wife's drinking on family life, it has been found that teenage children of a drinking father take an avoider role and withdraw from the family to a greater extent than the children of drinking mothers (McLachlan, Walderman, and Thomas 1973). Where the mother is the drinking parent, her role as the pivot and emotional focus of the family is impaired and children feel keenly the loss of mother love and attention. 'Physical functions of domestic organisation may not be performed and if the tasks are not taken over by older children, husbands are often at a loss to know how to cope' (Lawrence and Cran 1987:64). Also, if the mother is the non-excessively drinking parent, she may focus her energies on the drinker and deny the children her emotional attention inadvertently. Cork found that children:

> seem to feel the rejection of their non-alcoholic mother more keenly than that of their alcoholic father. It was as though they saw him as someone with a handicap and so believed that he could not help treating them as he did. They tended to make excuses for him that they did not make for the non-alcoholic parent.
>
> (Cork 1969)

How the family can be helped

A family unit with an alcohol problem will be experiencing a lot of stress, varying degrees of hardship, and may be extremely unstable. Lawrence and Cran (1987:68) suggest that there are two possible ways forward at this point. Either the family reorganizes itself by working around the drinker and excluding him, or the drinker 'recovers' and the family reorganizes and includes him in its new way of functioning. This view can be extended to increase the range of possible outcomes for the family and the drinker (see Table 8.1). Workers can provide support at this stage by discussing and exploring possible outcomes for the family with its individual members. If the family feels that change is an achievable, desirable outcome, workers can facilitate the process of change by discussing altered roles, status, and expectations with family members and by helping them to clarify what they are each prepared to contribute to the process. Lawrence and Cran point out the need for workers to offer continued support to all the family members during the period of change:

> Achieving a new balance in the family system which acknowledges the functioning of a former drinking member requires delicate adjustment. Other family members will have assumed roles, status and expectations during the drinking phase to compensate for the deficiency imposed by the drinker, and may resent, and attempt to sabotage, any new dynamic which threatens their position.
>
> (Lawrence and Cran 1987)

Table 8.1 Range of possible outcomes for drinker and family

Drinker changes behaviour ———————	Family does not change
Drinker changes behaviour ———————	Family also changes
Drinker does not change ———————	Family changes
Drinker does not change ———————	Family does not change

They also warn workers not to withdraw support too soon 'immediately there appears some semblance of "normality" or achievement of status quo'. Once a new level of stability has been attained, workers may need to help families re-establish links with the outside community. A major review of the work undertaken with families where alcohol causes problems, concludes that, if the outcome of change on the part of both the drinker and the family is accepted and agreed, workers have room for optimism. 'There is strong indication that family treatment for alcoholism can be successful. . . . Treatment which begins with the family is apparently successful in producing change both in the alcoholic and in the family' (Janzen 1977:114–30).

In his study of 100 couples where the husbands were undergoing treatment for drinking problems, Orford *et al.* (1976:318–39) asked the wives how they coped with their husbands' drinking. The replies were varied and Orford divided them into two sets of coping strategies, each associated with a good or poor prognosis seen in terms of the husbands' drinking over 12 months (see Table 8.2).

Table 8.2 Coping strategies of wives of problem drinkers associated with a good/poor prognosis

Good prognosis	Poor prognosis
Starting a row when he gets drunk	Telling him he must leave
Making him feel small or ridiculous in public	Feeling you could not face going home
Pouring some of his drink away	Refusing to share a bed with him
Drinking some of his drink yourself	Consulting about getting legal separation or divorce
Hitting him	Hiding valuables or possessions
Going out to fetch him home	Keeping the children out of his way
	Feeling too frightened to do anything

Source: Orford, J. (1979).

On the whole, it was the coping behaviours which seemed to involve engagement with the husband, even if the engagement was a stormy one, which indicated the better prognosis, and coping behaviours which involved avoidance or disengagement which held the worst prognosis.

(Orford 1979)

Although workers should remain alert and sensitive to the needs and circumstances of each family, they should appreciate that coping strategies based on avoidance and withdrawal appear to be associated with a poor prognosis. It may be helpful to explain this to family members and to explore other ways of coping that allow them to interact with the drinker, to remain engaged with him, and to increase the opportunities for change.

Throughout this process, it will be helpful if family members continue to give clear, consistent messages about the unacceptability of the drinking behaviour. In her book *Off the Hook. Coping with Addiction*, Helen Bethune (1985) gives clear guidelines for parents coping with a child's addiction to alcohol or drugs. The guidelines are equally applicable to families coping with an adult's drinking problem. Bethune points out the negative effects of colluding with, nagging, or criticizing the drinker and urges those who are trying to cope to decide on priorities and to clarify what is really important in terms of the drinker's behaviour. Instead of collusion, she recommends that family members state their feelings truthfully, set limits for behaviour, and stick to them. If messages about acceptable/unacceptable behaviour are given inconsistently, the drinker will not be convinced of the need for change. It may be tempting for the drinker's spouse or partner to nag or criticize, but Bethune warns 'the self-fulfilling prophecy tells us that if we expect the worst from people, by constantly criticising and carping, that's exactly what we'll make happen' (1985:85). Constant criticism will simply provide the drinker with an opportunity to 'switch off' mentally and to continue the drinking behaviour and resist change. Workers can help family members identify the aspects of the drinker's behaviour they find most difficult to tolerate and those they would most like to see change and encourage them to concentrate on these rather than being side-tracked by less

Table 8.3 Suggestions on how family members might respond to a drinking problem

Do's	Don'ts
Learn the facts about alcohol and dispel myths	Don't be ashamed or hide the problem from the family, the doctor, etc.
Be willing to offer help or support when effort is shown	Don't take on responsibility for the drinker
Try to understand and control your own emotions	Don't be baited into argument or retaliation
Seek personal relaxation and leisure activities	Don't become preoccupied with the drinking or allow life to revolve solely around the drinker
Let the drinker know you care but are not prepared to tolerate destructive drinking	Don't make idle threats, nag, cover up, or clear up
Seek advice/help from a professional worker or a support agency	Don't isolate the drinker
Inform the drinker of the unhappy and ill effects of his behaviour	Don't hide or dump bottles or evidence of heavy drinking
Encourage desirable behaviour and reward effort to change	Don't demand or accept unrealistic promises
Try to be patient and compassionate	Don't drink along with the drinker
Remove drinking-support props and discourage heavy drinking	Don't accept or allow personal or child abuse

important issues. Table 8.3 contains some suggestions that may be h
for workers wanting to encourage a positive response to a drink
problem.

Alcohol education and the family

Just as the drinker needs to understand some of the basic facts about
alcohol (see Chapter 7), so too will family members benefit from a clearer
understanding of the properties of alcohol, its effects, and functional use.
The worker may need to encourage them to consider their own roles
in the problem situation (persecutor, rescuer, victim) and explore ways
of changing or modifying those roles. Techniques used in alcohol education can help people overcome 'blind spots' where they have become
so accustomed to perceiving and reacting to a problem situation in a given
way that they are unable to contemplate change. As Egan (1986) points
out 'old and often comfortable frames of reference keep them locked
into self-defeating patterns of thinking and behaving' (p. 41). Helping
clients to achieve a better understanding of their problem situation, its
effects and their individual contributions to it is the first step in the process
of identifying how and where changes can be made. In getting basic
information about alcohol across to family members, the worker may
use leaflets, books, or articles, but should also be prepared to spend time
explaining points and discussing issues with individuals.

The worker should also guard against being drawn into the 'drinking
game' at this stage (see Chapter 3) or taking responsibility for either
the drinker or the family. If family members pose questions such as:

'Why does he keep on doing it?'

'Why doesn't she ever listen?'

'Why haven't things improved?'

the worker may feel he has a responsibility to offer some explanation
but, in doing so, would actually diminish the chances of the drinker and
family members taking some degree of responsibility for the problem
situation themselves. If a situation has not improved, the worker's role
is to help clarify why and to explore how change could be effected rather
than attempt to achieve change on behalf of the family.

Having ensured that family members have a factual information base
about alcohol, the worker can use various strategies for promoting the

process of change within the family situation. Some of the strategies may already be familiar — they are applicable to many problem situations — and should be used selectively and flexibly, depending on the stage family members are at and what they want to consider and discuss. They can be used with individuals or with family groups.

1. *Brainstorming* is a way of generating an agenda to work with. It is useful if family members find it difficult to be clear about issues or to discuss them openly. For example, brainstorming can be used to look at:

   (a) *Problems.* 'What bothers you about . . .?
   (b) *Positive aspects.* 'What are the good things about . . .?'
   (c) *Solutions.* 'What could we do to . . .?'

In encouraging people to think freely and imaginatively it is important to accept all suggestions without comment or criticism no matter how unrealistic or exaggerated they may seem. The process of sifting and identifying comes at a later stage. Brainstorming simply elicits responses and helps people to overcome blind spots and think more creatively than they are, perhaps, used to if they are locked into a problem.

Family members can write down what their brainstorms generate, or the worker can note down the suggestions.

2. *Ranking and categorizing* helps to increase individuals' self-awareness and encourages them to reach decisions. It is useful to isolate the criteria they use to make those decisions and this is an important step in the clarification process. The worker could take several issues raised in the brainstorm and ask family members to rank and categorize them.

   (a) *List of problems.* 'Which do you find most/least difficult to tolerate?'
   (b) *List of positive aspects.* 'Which are the most/least important to you?'
   (c) *List of solutions.* 'Which actions could you take most/least easily?'

3. *Solving problems and making decisions* are useful ways of ensuring that people accept some degree of responsibility for a problem situation and that they play an active role in any possible solution. There are four basic steps to follow:

    (a) Discuss the problem and clarify what you would like to change.

    (b) Brainstorm ways of achieving the desired changes and weigh up the pros and cons and likely consequences of each solution.

    (c) Agree on a solution and use it consistently over an agreed period of time.

    (d) Evaluate it and discuss whether it worked and was helpful. If not, go back to step (b) and pick a different solution.

4. *Identifying positives and negatives* can help people explore issues in greater depth and appreciate their complexity. Few issues can be seen in stark terms of black and white. Identifying the good and bad things about a particular issue will help individuals raise levels of awareness about both their own and others' points of view. This technique can also help people identify behaviour or attitudes in need of change. Individuals should be encouraged to consider a particular aspect of the drinking problem and identify what is good and bad about it. They should then do the same from the drinker's point of view. What do they imagine he finds good and bad about it? If the responses are very different, both the drinker and family members should be encouraged to work towards a position where the positive and negative aspects are more evenly balanced.

5. *Setting goals* is a useful way of taking people past the decision stage towards more constructive patterns of behaviour. Egan (1986) says 'goal setting is the central point of the helping process' (p. 248) and it can help to focus individuals' attention and action. It directs their energies towards something that can be achieved and prevents them engaging in aimless behaviour. In setting goals, it is important to ensure that they are realistic and achievable, that an adequate timescale is adopted and that people understand the individual role they are to play and how their personal contriubution will influence the outcome.

6. *Self-monitoring* helps people to keep a detailed account of their behaviour. Subsequent analysis can highlight areas that can be improved or it may clarify specific situations and circumstances that cause difficulties. Self-monitoring in the form of a diary or a regularly kept record will also provide a base line against which progress can be measured.

Alcohol-education exercises

The following section contains some practical exercises that may be useful for work in the family setting and are relevant both to family members and the drinker. As in Chapter 7, the exercises are not set out in any particular order and are not intended to be used as a developmental sequence. Workers should decide on what is relevant and helpful to the family (raising self-awareness and awareness of others, identifying and clarifying problem areas, focusing on specific problems) and choose an appropriate exercise.

Raising self-awareness and awareness of others

Is it O.K. for someone like me?

Purpose To raise individuals' awareness of their drinking habits. To encourage individuals to be aware of other people's opinions. To highlight possible areas of conflict or concern.

Materials/preparation Copies of 'Is it OK for someone like me?'

Method Explain that the questionnaire should be completed by ticking answers to the questions in column 1 'I think it's OK.' Then column 2 'My spouse/partner thinks it's OK' and column 3 'My family thinks it's OK'.

   The examples given are not good and bad reasons to drink, but will help to highlight possible areas of conflict or disagreement within families about drinking habits and behaviour. Discuss the results with family members and encourage them to consider their own behaviour.

Swapping roles

Purpose To help individuals appreciate other people's points of view.

Materials/preparation This exercise is most useful to the drinker and the spouse/partner, although older family members could also take part. Ask the family to think of one particular problem situation they experienced recently.

Table 8.4 Is it OK for someone like me?

	I think it's OK	My spouse/ partner thinks it's OK	My family thinks it's OK
To go to the pub for a drink at night			
To go for a drink after work			
To drink in my lunch-hour			
To drink before starting work			
To have wine with a meal			
To have a nightcap			
To drink while watching TV			
To drink more at weekends because I don't have to get up so early			
To drink on my own			
To drink when I am depressed			
bored			
frustrated			
angry			

Source: Adapted from Simnett, Wright and Evans (1983).

Method Once the problem situation has been agreed and defined, ask the drinker and the spouse/partner to swap roles and to imagine they are the other person while they answer these questions:

'Why did the problem arise?'

'Whose fault was it?'

'How was I feeling at the time?'

'What did I contribute to the problem?'

'Positively? Negatively?

'How did I deal with the problem?'

'What other ways(s) could I have dealt with it?'

Ensure each person has a chance to speak without being interrupted and then encourage discussion. Ask family members how accurate the descriptions were. Did they sum up their feelings? Did they provide any new insights? How does it feel to be sitting in another person's place? What did they learn?

Identifying and clarifying problem areas

What is going wrong, what is going right?

Purpose To help individuals identify problematic areas in their lives. To encourage individuals to be aware of their resources and successes as well as their problems and failures.

Materials/preparation Paper and pen.

Method Without referring specifically to the problem-drinking situation, ask individuals to jot down things that are going right in their lives and things that are going wrong or could, at least, be going better. The ideas do not need to be in any order of importance but, to stress the positive, there should be as many things going right as there are things going wrong. For example:

What is going right	*What is going wrong*
I have some good friends	I have a negative attitude towards myself
I am reasonably healthy	I worry about the future
I have a good job and salary	The family is always arguing

Encourage individuals to share their lists with others and to appreciate the positive as well as the negative aspects. (It may be helpful to follow this with an exercise on focusing. See p. 137–9).

Decision balance sheet

Purpose To help individuals clarify the consequences of a particular course of action. To help individuals appreciate the costs and benefits of a particular course of action. To help individuals clarify their own feelings.

Materials/preparation Copies of decision balance sheet (Table 8.5).

Method Ask individuals to define the course of action they propose to take (i.e. cut down on drinking, be more communicative, stop nagging). Encourage them to complete the decision balance sheet considering both themselves and their spouse/partner. Discuss the results. Will the course of action achieve what they want? If not, why not? Is it acceptable to them personally? Is it acceptable to their spouse/partner? If there are differences, what might the outcome be if the action is undertaken anyway? Is there a possible compromise?

Table 8.5 The decision balance sheet

If I choose this course of action:

(a) *For myself*

Gains:	Acceptable to me because:	Not acceptable to me because:
Losses:	Acceptable to me because:	Not acceptable to me because:

(b) *For my spouse/partner*

Gains:	Acceptable to me because:	Not acceptable to me because:
Losses:	Acceptable to me because:	Not acceptable to me because:

Focusing on specific problems

Which issue to explore?

Purpose To help individuals decide which issues are important and whether to focus on them or not. To apply criteria to a chosen issue that will help in its exploration and clarification.

137

Materials/preparation Copy of criteria for exploration and clarification (Table 8.6). Paper and pen.

Method Ask individuals to jot down their main concerns about their given situation. What are the main problems and difficulties they face? Which issues seem to come up again and again? Encourage each individual to consider his list and help him to apply the criteria set out in Table 8.6. Discuss the results and compare with other family members' lists. Can the family, as a whole, agree on one or two main concerns or problems that each member would agree to tackle?

Table 8.6 Criteria to explore and clarify problems

Severity or urgency — does this problem need immediate attention because of the distress it causes you or others and/or because of its frequency or uncontrollability?

Importance — is this an issue that is important to you, important enough to discuss and act on?

Timing — do you feel it is time to do something about it?

Complexity — is this problem a manageable part of a larger or more complex problem situation? Can it be divided into more manageable parts?

Effect — if this problem is handled in a better way, might it lead to improvement in other areas of your life?

Control — is this problem under your control? To manage it more effectively, do you have to act or do you have to influence others to act?

Cost-effectiveness — do the benefits of handling this problem more effectively outweigh the costs in terms of time and effort?

Source: Adapted from Egan (1985).

Concentric circles

Purpose To help individuals brainstorm issues and concerns. To encourage individuals to categorize them and put them into perspective.

Materials/preparation Paper and pen (see Figure 8.3).

Method Encourage individuals to brainstorm one of the following related to their problem situation:

1. Things I find it hard to cope with.
2. My personal strengths and weaknesses.

3. Good and bad points about my marriage/relationship/family.

Using the examples given in Figure 8.3, encourage individuals to put their suggestions in an appropriate place within the concentric circles. If other family members complete the same exercise, compare the results and discuss the issues that have been placed inside the smallest circle. What are the main issues and concerns?

Figure 8.3 Concentric Circles

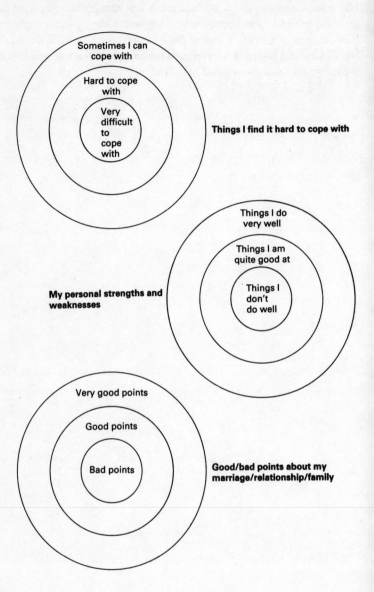

Alcohol education: getting over the difficulties

Chapter nine

Overcoming obstacles and difficulties

Alcohol education, like any other skill, will benefit from practice and workers using alcohol education regularly with clients and patients will find that the processes become absorbed rapidly into their everyday working routine. They may, however, encounter certain barriers or obstacles that are worth considering in advance so that they are neither side-tracked nor taken aback and are ready to overcome them with well thought-out strategies.

In coming to terms with his drinking, the drinker will find himself in a situation in which he is expected to confront his behaviour and the effect it has on others and to make decisions and act upon them. He sees the need for change and, although encouraged and supported, may feel vulnerable and frightened. The prospect of effecting change with its possible risks of failure may serve to demotivate him and may therefore result in inaction, even though the current situation is far from satisfactory. Alternatively, he may attempt some form of action to bring about change but, finding that his hopes and expectations are not fulfilled or that the effort is simply too great to sustain, he may abandon the attempt and revert back to the original behaviour. The result could be confusion, disillusionment, instability, and loss of confidence. At this stage, the worker should ensure that lines of communication are kept open and that rapport is maintained. This will help to reduce the confusion and will provide a level of stability from which to build up personal confidence and optimism. The worker's role is to encourage and support rather than to take responsibility for any apparent 'failures' arising from attempts to change behaviour. The client may also need help to assess what did not work and why, and how these difficulties can be overcome in the future.

In his chaper 'The challenge of painful and unpleasant emotions', Snell

(1987) says of those who are presented with opportunities for personal development, 'that they will experience a measure of emotional pain or discomfort resulting from both the new insight they may gain into themselves and the very process of moving from the known and familiar into the unknown' (p. 63). The worker should acknowledge these feelings and resist the temptation to ignore them, gloss over them or minimize their importance. Snell adds 'to seek to prevent such pain in such circumstances is tantamount to attempting to block personal development, as the risk of some pain appears to be inherent in learning of this nature, rather like growing pains some children experience.' He puts forward four main strategies for addressing emotional pain and discomfort: prevention, masking, soothing, and working with and through feelings. These strategies can be applied to the feelings of individuals trying to confront and/or change their drinking behaviour and an assessment made of the benefits and limitations of each strategy.

1. *Prevention*. Workers using a prevention strategy in relation to clients' emotional pain and discomfort will try to anticipate when it might occur and what might trigger it, and will attempt to avoid such circumstances altogether. Owing to 'the impossibility of predicting and controlling human experience or action, or of catering for the diversity of ideas and social values' (Snell 1987:65), the strategy is flawed and limited. Workers should aim to empower clients/patients to direct their own experiences, rather than attempting to control or predict them.

2. *Masking*. An approach that drowns out unpleasant, negative emotions by amplifying pleasant, positive ones. The client, however, may feel that his anxieties are not being acknowledged and that the worker is not listening to him. He may not have many pleasant, positive emotions that can be amplified or may need the presence of the negative ones as a reminder of the need to change the situation.

3. *Soothing*. Painful, uncomfortable feelings such as anguish, despair, suffering, and anxiety are edged out and replaced with calm, solace, and relaxation. This strategy may be seen as patronizing by the client, who may find it frustrating when he needs to vent negative feelings.

4. Working with and through feelings. Emotional pain and discomfort are used constructively to promote learning, understanding, and development. This strategy acknowledges both the feelings and their importance

to the client and helps him address the feelings rather than remaining constrained and disempowered by them.

John Dewey identified two distinct phases in the learning process that are interdependent and necessary if change is to take place. In his chapter 'Experience and thinking' he notes:

> Mere activity does not constitute experience. It is dispersive, centrifugal, dissipating. Experience as trying involves change, but change is meaningless transition unless it is consciously connected with the return wave of consequences which flow from it. When an activity is continued into the undergoing of consequences, when the change made by action is reflected back into a change made by us, the mere flux is loaded with significance. We learn something.
>
> (Dewey 1916)

Workers should aim to raise clients' awareness of the learning process and should encourage them to reflect on what has been achieved. This may take time and patience as, in general, people are not encouraged to give themselves mental 'pats on the back' or to sit back and reflect on their good points and achievements. The upper sections of Maslow's (1943) hierarchy of human needs (see Chapter 3) deal with love, esteem and self-actualisation and he writes 'satisfaction of the esteem needs leads to feelings of self-confidence, worth, strength, capability, and adequacy of being useful and necessary in the world'.

Communication barriers

Progress and change may not be achieved in easy stages and workers may discover barriers to communication that prevent them getting the message across or that limit clients'/patients' ability to understand or retain information. Throughout working relationships, workers should remain sensitive to possible blocks to communication and, if the progress anticipated is not achieved, should not always conclude that this is due to resistance or lack of motivation on the part of the client. The following list gives some possible communication barriers that, given some forethought and a little patience, should not prove insurmountable.

1. The cultural gap between worker and client/patient.
2. Limited client/patient receptiveness.

3. Limited understanding and/or memory.
4. Contradictory messages.
5. Language barriers.
6. The worker not convinced about the value of alcohol education.
7. Negative responses and/or attitudes towards the worker.
8. The client's/patient's lack of motivation.

There are no easy solutions or short cuts that can be used to overcome obstacles and workers should be prepared to exercise patience. It is important that they maintain an awareness of such problems and use their skills to improve the level of communication with clients and patients. It is more likely to be a case of whittling away at a problem rather than attempting to solve it with one stroke.

The cultural gap between the worker and client/patient

If a client/patient has a different ethnic background, the worker should be sensitive to different religious and cultural beliefs and expectations. The client and his family may have a different system of values (see Chapter 3), which affects their attitudes to the use of alcohol and to problem drinking. They may find it extremely difficult to admit that alcohol is causing problems if its use is not culturally approved and there may be fear of bringing shame on the family. The worker should aim to be seen as someone who can be trusted and who is ready to offer family support rather than someone who has come to judge or criticize. It is important to remember however, that there may be decades of conditioning to overcome and it is unlikely that such barriers can be broken down overnight.

Limited client/patient receptiveness

There may be several reasons why a client/patient does not appear to be interested in or concerned about his current situation. He may not value himself or his health positively or may feel helpless to change the situation. He may be worn down by emotional pain, confusion, and desperation and may find it dificult to trust anyone. The worker should use patience and stay with these feelings and not try to ignore them or minimize their disabling effect.

Limited understanding and/or memory

A client/patient may have difficulty in speaking or understanding English, may be of limited intelligence, may have a poor memory, or may be illiterate. The worker should assess the difficulties posed by the language barrier (see language barriers, p. 147–8) and, if he decides to continue with the client/patient, should avoid using jargon or idiomatic English. If the client/patient has a poor memory, the worker could ask him to write down two or three things they have agreed to do. If he is illiterate, the worker could ask him to repeat two or three key points. It is important to be clear about what has been agreed between the worker and client and to ensure that he understands and is committed to any plan of action.

Contradictory messages

The worker should be aware of the possible influence of family members and friends on the drinker and his behaviour. They may contradict what the worker says, especially if any of the proposed changes to the drinker's behaviour affect them personally. The worker should be clear about the messages given and could leave written information such as leaflets and booklets to support work that has been done with the client/patient on drinking and driving, safe limits for drinking, calorific values, or alcohol absorption and metabolization.

Language barriers

If the client/patient has a limited understanding of English, the worker should decide whether a working relationship is practical and possible. Henley (1979) provides some useful guidelines for health professionals engaged with clients/patients whose grasp of English is limited. These include speaking slowly and repeating phrases using the *same words*. This will give the client/patient more time to understand what is being said, rather than having to understand new words and phrases. It is important to use plain English and avoid idioms that may be confusing. The worker should avoid closed questions that require only a one-word answer and should encourage the client/patient to repeat key points or phrases to ensure they have been understood. To help in establishing rapport with the client/patient, the worker might find it helpful to learn one or two key words and phrases in his language and use them to bridge the gap. (Multicultural education centres run by local education authorities may be able to help.)

The worker not convinced about the value of alcohol education

Research in psychotherapy has highlighted the importance of the worker's commitment and enthusiasm in any therapeutic relationship (Malan 1963; Truax and Wargo 1966). If the worker is not personally convinced about the value of alcohol education, that ambivalence will be communicated to the client/patient who will, in turn, devalue it. Harwin and Hunt (1979) emphasize how important it is for the worker to 'demonstrate confidence in the method of work' used and 'commitment to the client' p. 138. Confidence in the method of work comes from a sound grasp of its rationale, goals, and techniques and commitment to the client arises from 'the principle that every client is an acceptable and worthwhile individual'. By using alcohol education, the worker is giving information to the client and teaching him skills to make conscious, informed decisions about behaviour. If he continues to drink in a way that causes problems, it is a personal choice and responsibility and should not be seen as either failure on the part of the worker or on the part of alcohol education.

Negative attitudes and/or responses to the worker

The client/patient may see the health professional as a threat or as an outsider who has come to moralize or pass judgement or criticism. He may feel angry at needing professional help or may fear that change is expected or that he will have to modify or give up pleasurable habits. The worker should try to understand these feelings and encourage the client/patient to express them. If negative attitudes and responses are maintained, the worker may confront them directly using the four stages in challenging behaviour set out in Chapter 7.

The client's/patient's lack of motivation

In the face of client's/patient's continued negative attitudes and responses, the worker may conclude that he lacks motivation. Sterne and Pitman (1965:44–55) investigated the concept of motivation in work with alcoholics and recognized its importance in determining behavioural outcome. They also noted that client's 'lack of motivation' and 'resistance' was felt by professional workers to be a major obstacle in therapy. Ripple (1964), however, points out that the degree of motivation or resistance exhibited by a client or patient is likely to change during the course of a working relationship. If the worker has decided to withdraw from the relationship because he is not convinced of the client's motivation, no changes can occur and the offer of help becomes conditional on the worker's interpretation of the client's genuineness and willingness to alter behaviour. The client may appear ambivalent and remain unconvinced about a possible solution to his problems. The worker should allow the client to voice the fear and anxieties that often underlie denial and evasion. If he feels both hopeless and helpless in the face of problems, the worker should show confidence in the ability to help him find a solution and commitment to helping him improve the quality of life. The drinker will find it easier to admit that there is a problem if he believes there is a possible solution.

Resistance and reluctance

Workers may encounter clients/patients who are reluctant to engage in a working relationship and who remain resistant to change. Some clients/patients do not accept that they need help or are resentful because they have been forced to see a health and welfare professional, perhaps as a result of pressure and threats from a third party. They may show their resentment by remaining aloof or refusing to co-operate with the worker. Alternatively, they may talk freely and openly about 'safe' issues which allow them to avoid discussing more sensitive, emotive or meaningful areas of their lives. Egan describes these clients/patients as those:

> who feel abused; who are resentful; who only talk about safe or low priority issues; who sabotage the helping process by being overly co-operative; who are directly or indirectly uncooperative; who set unrealistic goals and then use them as an excuse for not working; who unwarrantedly blame others or the social settings and systems of their lives for their troubles; who show no willingness to establish a relationship with the helper; who do not work very hard at changing their behaviour; who play games with helpers; who are slow to take responsibility for themselves; who are either testy or actually abusive or belligerent.
>
> (Egan 1986:145)

He also reminds us that there are degrees of resistance and clients/patients are unlikely to display all these extremes of attitudes and behaviour.

The area of resistance can become the short-term focus for the work between the worker and client but, if recognized and dealt with, a new focus can be established. Brandes and Ginnis (1986) see resistance as an important part of the learning process and say 'since resistance is viewed as a necessary step in the process of change, it is not regarded as a deterrent p. 85. Other writers see resistance as a positive sign of struggle and awareness within the client/patient and Redl (1966:216) states 'resistance is an unavoidable process in every effective treatment, for that part of the personality that has an interest in the survival of the pathology actively protests each time therapy comes close to inducing a successful change.' As with other negative feelings, the client's/patient's reluctance or resistance should be acknowledged and explored if he is to pass beyond that stage with confidence. A large part of being adult revolves around independence and the ability and opportunity to be self-directing. A client, although in difficulty, will not appreciate an over-bearing, authoritarian approach and, unless he sees a benefit for himself and has the skills needed to effect change, he is unlikely even to attempt it.

Rather than seeing reluctance and resistance as barriers to communication or as evidence of the client's lack of motivation, workers may find it helpful to differentiate between the two concepts and explore what lies behind them before going on to develop coping strategies. Reluctant clients are those who do not want outside help or who have been co-erced into accepting it by a spouse, partner, or employer. They need to understand that an offer of help made by a worker — a listening ear, counselling, personal support, or education and information — is freely offered and is not conditional on compliance or behaviour change. Resistant clients may have overcome their initial reluctance but resist giving themselves fully to the helping process at one or several stages. They may agree to explore their drinking problems, to take part in a problem-solving process, and to set new behavioural goals but only implement them in a half-hearted manner. In working with such clients/patients, it is helpful to understand some of the more common causes of reluctance and resistance. These can be divided into internal and external factors.

Where internal factors are at play, the client is suspicious, fears what is unfamiliar, and does not understand the purpose of the relationship between himself and the worker. He may fear loss of face if he requests or accepts help from an outside source and may realize a sense of personal power and control in actively resisting a professional worker or a helping agency. Again, this need not be seen as an obstacle in the helping process. Riordan, Matheny, and Harris (1978) suggest that it may be a healthy sign as 'clients are grasping for a share in the control of their destiny' p. 8. External factors may arise from bad experiences with outside helpers and agencies in the past resulting in loss of faith in and negative attitudes towards the helping process. Clients may have a history of rebelliousness that they maintain in the form of resistance. Rebellion and/or resistance may have become their way of responding in difficult situations. Alternatively, resistance may simply be related to age, sex, race, social class, upbringing, or to a genuine fear of change. An older client may find it hard to accept help from a younger worker or a man may resent help being offered to him by a woman. Workers will respond in different ways to reluctance and resistance but should aim to avoid being distracted by it or becoming irritated or impatient. Resistance should be faced openly and explored but should not give rise to a power struggle between the worker and client.

Egan puts forward several productive approaches for dealing with resistance that include:

1. *See some resistance as normative.* It can be a sign of struggle within the client and an indication of his/her self-affirmation.

2. *Look for avoidance underlying resistance.* Aim to engage the client in the helping process and seek incentives which will help him/her move beyond resistance. Show him/her how the helping process can be positive and rewarding.

3. *Accept and work with resistance.* Do not ignore it or become intimidated by it. Help the client to work through the emotions associated with resistance. Explain how you experience and feel about his/her resistance and model openness yourself.

4. *Begin with small goals.* By beginning with realistic goals which the client can achieve, you will reduce the risk of him/her setting unrealistic ones and then opting out of the helping process when they are not achieved.

5. *Use others as resources.* There may be other sources of help, support and influence in your client's life who can help him/her work through resistance.

(Egan 1986:149–52)

It will also help if the worker remains realistic and flexible in the approach to the client's resistance and is aware of both personal and professional limits. By inviting the client to participate in every step of the helping process and in all the decision-making, the worker will establish a relationship based on mutual respect. This will help to prevent the client seeing the helping process as an imposition or a punishment and should enable him to work through and come to terms with feelings of resistance and reluctance.

Monitoring and encouraging progress

This should be a two-way process in which both worker and client participate. The worker should not necessarily judge progress but should provide guidance and support and help the client recognize progress.

Feedback can confirm that the client is on course and is moving successfully through various stages of an action plan. Alternatively, it can be corrective if he needs help to get back on course. Exploring the possible consequences of action or inaction on the part of the client may serve to increase motivation and encouraging him to monitor progress will help him to take more responsibility for it.

Education for crisis or relapse

When working with clients or patients it is always possible that a crisis may occur or that part of an intended action plan will not work and there may be a tendency to lapse into old, familiar ways of coping or responding. Crises often develop as a response to sudden or unusual stress in a client's life such as family rows, illness or death within the family, break-up of relationships, or legal or financial problems. Heavy drinking may be used on some occasions to give vent to aggression or anger and the worker may need to cope first with the practical issues involved. Some clients only seek outside help when a situation, which may have been simmering for some time, suddenly erupts. Workers can use crisis-intervention skills to help clients at this stage and can also encourage them to accept that a crisis or lapse is a possibility. They should help them to develop contingency plans to deal with the situation. Plans do not need to be overly complex as it is important not to get lost in details or overload clients/patients with too many things to do. Egan writes:

Having back-up also helps clients develop more responsibility. If they see that a plan is not working, they have to decide whether

to try the contingency plan. Back-up plans need not be complicated. A counselor might merely ask, 'If that doesn't work, then
what will you do?'

(Egan 1986:325–6)

Relapse should be an issue between worker and client before it occurs
and the emphasis should be on maintaining contact and seeing it as a
learning experience. It is vital for both the worker and the client not
to see a lapse as an indication of total failure that invalidates any other
attempts to change. Hunt and Harwin (1979) highlight the advantages
of evolving new awareness and applying the lessons learned to new situations and state 'crisis theory, which has its roots in ego psychology,
perceives a state of crisis as containing the potential for personal growth'
(p. 135). Implementing any new skill takes time and practice and learning
often takes place when mistakes have been made. When learning to ride
a bicycle, it would be unusual if the rider did not experience one or two
precarious moments or tumbles during the learning process.

Rapoport (1965) saw crisis as 'a catalyst that disturbs old habits and
evokes new responses. . . . The challenge it provokes may bring forth
new coping mechanisms which serve to strengthen the individual's
adaptive capacity.' A return to previous patterns of drinking may occur
in response to extra stress, boredom, deeply felt emotions, or a feeling
that no progress is being made. Alternatively, a special occasion, meeting
old (drinking) friends or the physical and psychological urges arising
from withdrawal from alcohol might precipitate a crisis situation. If crisis
does arise, the drinker may be panicked and confused. The confusion
may be so great that new coping skills are temporarily forgotten and
he is unable to formulate any plans for action. The resulting inaction
increases the sense of confusion and failure and leads to depression. At
this point, the drinker feels he is on a treadmill and needs help to bring
the problem into focus, decide what to tackle first, and gain some degree
of control over the situation.

Prochaska and Di Clemente (1982; 1983) studied both the process
of change and the stages within it undergone by 900 people who gave
up smoking. The model of change that they developed is applicable to
those trying to change their drinking behaviour. They suggest that
individuals are at different stages in their willingness or preparedness
to change (see Figure 9.1) and that, for many people attempting to alter
their behaviour, relapse is common. In the *precontemplation* stage, the
individual may not be aware that his behaviour is causing problems and

153

it is not until acknowledgement of the link between behaviour and the problems that he enters the *contemplation* stage. At this point he begins to consider altering his behaviour and is said to move into the *determination* stage where a serious commitment to action is formulated. By implementing action or change, the drinker enters the *maintenance* stage in which he must constantly practise new skills to maintain new habits or behaviours. If successful, he leaves the system of change to *termination*, which would indicate a favourable outcome in terms of new behaviour and coping methods. Raistrick and Davidson (1987) point out, however, that for most people 'attempting to alter addictive behaviour, *relapse* is common, notably in the first six months or so' p. 146. Following relapse, the individual either enters the *precontemplation* stage again or thinks once more about altering his behaviour in the *contemplation* stage. In the *maintenance* stage there is always a risk of relapse, which the worker should discuss in advance with the client. It is essential to be prepared for setbacks and to incorporate some contingency measures into the contract between client and worker.

Figure 9.1 Stages of individual change

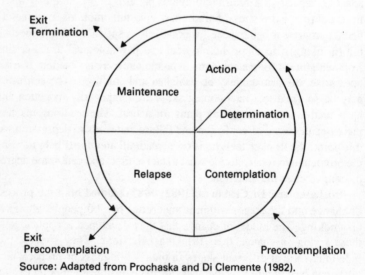

Source: Adapted from Prochaska and Di Clemente (1982).

Source: Adapted from Prochaska and Di Clemente (1982).

Egan (1986:162–9) proposes that workers can use the principles of focusing to help clients/patients deal with a crisis situation or come to terms with a relapse. Workers should be careful not to withdraw their support too quickly.

All too often worker support is withdrawn, immediately there appears some semblance of 'normality' or achievement of status quo. It is possible — even likely — that the pathology and tension of family interaction induces relapse, the reassumption by the drinker of former behaviour patterns and roles which, though maladaptive, hold a particular security status and acceptability for him or her within the family system.

(Lawrence and Cran 1987:68)

Workers can use the following principles of focusing to help clients/patients gain points of leverage in the management of problem or crisis situations and can encourage them to isolate influential factors in order to develop a more extended repertoire of coping techniques.

1. *If there is a crisis, first help the client manage the crisis.* The worker can provide help and support to the client enabling him to assess the situation, think more calmly and clearly about possible outcomes and decide on a course of action. This will help to reduce the client's confusion and feeling of helplessness and lack of control.

2. *Focus on issues that the client considers to be important.* In a crisis situation, the client may be particularly concerned about certain issues that the worker perceives as less important than others. If the worker rejects the client's perspective however, he runs the risk of the client rejecting any offer of help or support. At a moment of crisis or during or after relapse, the drinker wants someone to listen, to act as a sounding board and to remain involved and interested in him. By acting in this way, the worker will preserve the working relationship and the client's trust and can move on to other issues in due course.

3. *Begin with the problem that seems to be causing pain.* Pain and distress can act as a motivating force and may urge the client to seek help. Pain may also render clients vulnerable and open to influence or manipulation and workers should move cautiously. Rapoport (1965) saw crisis as a catalyst and, at this stage, a client may well be agreeable to change or may even become demanding and expect

155

the worker to reduce or remove the pain altogether. The worker should respect the client's vulnerability and help him to use the distress to explore possibilities of change. In this way, distress become a motivating force for the client rather than a source of confusion and inaction.

4. *Focus on an issue, however important, which the client is willing to work on.* Even when the immediate crisis has subsided, there are still many ways in which the worker can provide support and help clients work through problems and reduce them to manageable parts. After a relapse, the client may not be immediately willing to explore highly sensitive issues. He may experience a sense of failure and, although it is important for this to be explored and discussed, the worker may need to begin by looking at a less critical issue before moving on. The client's willingness to work on a particular issue, even though it may not be the most important, should be seen by the worker as a point of leverage on the problem situation.

5. *Begin with some manageable subproblem of a larger problem situation.* Clients experiening crisis situations may see problems as vague, overwhelming, and unmanageable. By helping a client divide large problems into more manageable parts and then working out priorities, the worker will increase the client's optimism and feeling that improvement and change is possible. Following on from this point, it makes sense to:

6. *Begin with a problem that can be managed relatively easily, one that shows promise of being successfully handled by the client.* Through managing a small part of a problem situation successfully, the client may feel empowered to tackle larger, more difficult issues. The initial experience of success with a simple problem may lead to the discovery of unknown or relatively unused coping abilities. Bobbe and Schaffer consider such discoveries as 'breakthrough projects' and say:

Success in carrying out change . . . even a rather moderate success — almost always reveals new opportunities for further change not visible before. These successes also produce new confidence and know-how about change. . . That is why we call these success experiences 'breakthrough projects' because they not only produce immediate progress but also generate the ingredients for additional accelerating progress.

(Bobbe and Schaffer 1968:7)

7. *Begin with a problem which, if handled, will lead to a general improvement in the client's overall condition.* In the face of a complex problem situation involving several issues, both the worker and client may find it difficult to know where to start. As the worker is not (or should not be) involved at an emotional, subjective level, he should consider the problem situation and assess whether there is a common factor or denominator that underlies the various issues. Can this factor be addressed? Is there a problem that, if handled successfully, may allow the client to generalize the learning experience and apply it to other, more difficult problems?

8. *When possible, move from less severe to more severe problems.* A client in crisis may not feel able, even with a worker's support, to tackle severe problems. He may need the reassurance and reinforcement of tackling more minor issues at first before moving on to more critical ones.

9. *Focus on a problem where the benefits of a solution will outweigh the costs.* Although not an excuse for ignoring or avoiding difficult problem situations, the worker should be aware and acknowledge that a solution to a problem that demands a great deal of work from both him and the client *must* also have a reasonable pay off or reward for both parties.

Although it is important to offer support to clients who are in crisis, workers should also be aware of the opportunities for change such a situation presents and should be wary of becoming simply 'a listening ear'. Listening to a client is certainly an important part of helping him deal with a crisis but the worker should move beyond that and, by using the principles outlined previously, help the client gain leverage on the problem, and try out new ways of dealing with it. The on-going relationship between the client and worker can also be used, once the immediate crisis has subsided, to generalize learning in one area of life to other, possibly more difficult areas so that the maximum benefit is gained from the learning experience.

Chapter ten

Increasing access to training

It is not only in the alcohol field that a broadly based preventive approach is being encouraged and developed. Similar developments can be seen in a wide range of health and social issues and spring from the concept of positive health as something more complex and more desirable than the simple absence of disease. At the same time, such approaches are also leading to greater provision of training for professionals — often carried out on a multidisciplinary basis — which permits exploration of one's individual and professional role in providing alcohol education for clients. There is increasing recognition of the role to be played by a wide range of health and welfare professionals in helping people and families affected by alcohol problems although there are some important considerations surrounding the provision of and access to appropriate and adequate training. D.L. Davies, formerly the Medical Director of the Alcohol Education Centre, London, said that more professionals would become involved in helping those with alcohol problems:

> if they saw the likely form of effective help to reside not in
> quasi-religious conversion, nor in specialised psychotherapy, nor
> in drug-regimes, but in the everyday application of the kind of
> sociological and psychological principles affecting learning and
> lifestyle of which they have already been taught something and
> could learn more.

(Davies 1979:109–10)

Even so, many professionals still feel the need for more specialized training related to alcohol misuse and its associated problems and this chapter looks at ways in which they might increase their own access to training and, also, ways in which their employing agencies or organizations might assist them.

How workers might help themselves

If professionals find, in their day-to-day work with clients, that they are meeting problems that they do not know how to tackle and about which they have received little or no training, it is reasonable to expect that they might look to their employers to provide training that will enable them to do their jobs more competently and effectively. In its report on *Alcohol — A Balanced View*, the Royal College of General Practitioners (1986) commented that 'the best education is based on the needs of the learner' p. 54 and, although this holds true as a general principle, it creates problems for organizations attempting to meet and prioritize the training needs of their employees. In this respect, in terms of persuading employers to provide the type of training they want, workers can do much to strengthen their case to ensure not only that the training is provided, but also that it is seen as a priority. In addition, there are some practical guidelines to follow to ensure that other sources of training outside the employing organization are identified and considered.

Practical guidelines to assess external training resources

1. *Professional groups.* Find out which professional groups exist locally and nationally and use their information networks to investigate possible training events. They are often in contact with specialist agencies and could provide specific information.

2. *Other professions.* Identify other professions that might have similar training needs and approach their training officers. Are there any training events planned that you could attend?

3. *Health education/promotion units.* Staff from health education/promotion units are often involved in providing and co-ordinating education and training on a wide range of health topics. Get in touch with a local unit and ask about what is planned for the future.

4. *Specialist agencies.* Identify specialist agencies in your locality that offer services to people with alcohol problems. Do they have any in-house sessions that you could attend or are they co-ordinating training with other agencies?

5. *Previous courses.* Consider any previous courses or training events that you or your colleagues have attended. If they were worthwhile, contact the organisers and trainers to see if further events are planned.

Practical guidelines to promote in-house training

After investigating the training that may be available to you outside your employing organization, you may find that, in the absence of anything appropriate, you have to rely on your employer to meet your training needs. Employers have a range of considerations to take into account when providing in-house training (see next section), and it is worth considering these before making your request.

1. *In-house training department.* It is worthwhile getting to know staff in the training department. Ask them what types of training are provided and what criteria *they* need to fulfill before mounting training events. Can you and other colleagues satisfy these criteria?

2. *Training outcomes.* Employers and training officers are more likely to be influenced by details of training outcomes than by repeated requests for the provision of training. Try to emphasize what you and your colleagues will be able to *do* as a result of the training. What are the pay offs for the organization?

3. *Staff-support systems.* Do other colleagues have similar training needs? Would you be prepared to report back on conferences and seminars you have attended? Would they do the same? If so, this could encourage the establishment of an informal staff-support system and could aid information exchange.

4. *Cross-professional links.* If an informal information exchange is established, could this be extended to other professional groups? This could lead to the cross-fertilisation of ideas and pooling of experiences, approaches, and techniques. If the joint demand for training was great enough, training departments might agree to collaborate in order to meet the consolidated training needs of various professional groups.

How employers might help

Employing organizations often find themselves in the position of having to achieve a certain degree of congruence between professional and organizational priorities. On the one hand, training may be seen as costly and time-consuming yet, on the other, workers must have appropriate training if they are to do their jobs efficiently and effectively. In their eagerness to explore new ground and to develop new skills, workers may tend to ignore or overlook the resource implications of training and, if their demands are not quickly responded to, may feel that their employers are inflexible and uncaring about their needs. If both parties take care to understand and appreciate the other's position, then it is more likely that a satisfactory conclusion and outcome will be reached.

In his book *Approaches to Training and Development*, Dugan Laird (1985) says 'in most organisations, at least four criteria must be considered: cost effectiveness, legal requirements, executive pressure, and population to be served' p. 60. To satisfy the criterion of cost-effectiveness, employing organizations might expect that the cost of training be reflected in its outcome so that the hours lost and the work left undone while employees undergo training is compensated for by their increased efficiency and effectiveness as a result. Some may argue that it is neither feasible nor desirable to work out costs for qualitative as opposed to quantitative provisions and, although this seems logical when faced with the problem of assessing the costs of the quality of care, the cost-effectiveness criterion remains a yardstick to be applied by employing organizations. If the cost of the solution is greater than the cost of the problem, some training needs may be allowed to slip down the list of organizational priorities.

In terms of legal or statutory requirements however, employing organizations have a duty to ensure that their workers receive appropriate training to enable them to accord with the law, regardless of whether such training is seen as cost-effective or not. Workers may be tempted to emphasize the importance of certain statutory responsibilities in an attempt to obtain the type of training input they feel they need. Executive pressure is a further issue to consider and may originate from both internal and external sources. Certain health and social issues seem to have innate topicality, whereas others achieve topicality because of increased media attention or the development of crisis situations. Some workers may even consider professionally provoked crises as an appropriate means of obtaining training provision and employers may find themselves in a position of having to respond. Such manoeuvres are not always simply manipulative, but may indicate very real concerns on the part of workers and an appreciation of the need to increase knowledge, examine attitudes, and develop and implement new skills. Finally, there is the criterion of

Figure 10.1 How employers might determine training needs

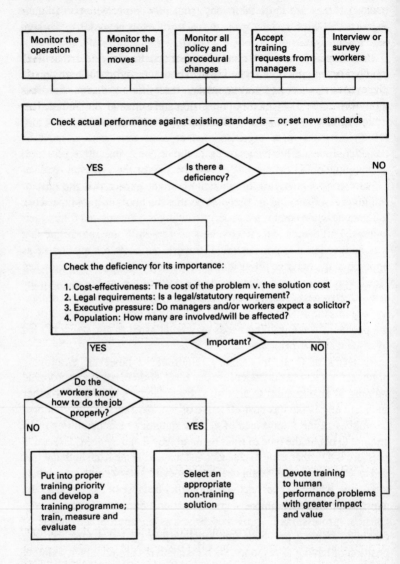

population. Laird (1985) says 'sometimes this means simply that training goes to the most extensive problem. Macro needs may take priority over micro needs', p. 61. Flexible employers, however, will also take the factors of influence and impact into account when prioritizing training needs (see Figure 10.1).

Occasionally, employers may find that training events are not well received or are poorly attended by workers and, rather than writing off the event as a waste of time and money, it may help to analyse the situation with a view to incorporating improvements in the future. The following list covers some of the main points to consider:

1. *Staff cover*. This presents a problem for both employers and employees. The former are concerned about the financial implications of providing cover while the latter are concerned about work that may be left undone and may accumulate during their absence at training events.

2. *Recruitment procedures*. If recruitment is not targetted at the appropriate groups, uptake of places at training events may be limited. It will be helpful to encourage dialogue between the trainers, professional workers, and their managers to ensure that training needs are specifically stated and accurately met.

3. *Management support*. Managers' perceptions of the value of training and the support they give to its subsequent implementation can vary. If workers feel they will not receive support after training to allow them to implement what they have learned, they may be reluctant to attend training events. Alternatively, there may be an unwillingness to be seen as the office or agency 'specialist' and take on *all* the work related to alcohol problems. Employers should consider the training needs of staff in both their short-term and strategic plans and should ensure that the physical and financial development of services also include a staff–development component.

Appraisal and assessment

Both employers and employees may find that either formal or informal appraisal and assessment sessions offer opportunities to discuss training needs. Workers should be encouraged to review their work performance and comment on how they perceive their professional development. Employers can assist by ensuring that workers understand clearly what is expected from them in terms of job performance and should be prepared to assess future training needs or indicate possible non-training solutions. It is important for both parties to acknowledge that training should not always be seen as reactive. Admittedly, training may help a worker improve his current performance but, in the proactive sense, it may also serve to prepare him for a new role or to take on new responsibilities or may allow the organization to grow and operate in new spheres and environments.

If employers are unable or unwilling (for whatever reason) to give an in-house response to workers' demands for training, they should at least make available and support a range of alternative solutions. Briefly, these might include some of the following:

1. *Modules from existing courses*. It may be appropriate for workers to attend small sections or modules of existing training courses and programmes offered by other organizations.

2. *Arranging special sessions*. Workers might benefit from an opportunity to discuss their concerns with others who are interested, find themselves in similar positions, or have had previous experience. Although no formal training takes place, everyone benefits from the exchange of experiences, ideas, and approaches.

3. *Self-study packs*. Materials may be available that could form the basis of self-study packs for workers. If not, approaches could be made to a variety of national or local organizations. (See section on 'Where to get further information' p. 165).

4. *Arranging visits*. Workers may feel a need to find out for themselves what takes place within specialist alcohol agencies. Vists can help to satisfy this natural curiosity and also can encourage information exchanges between specialist and generic workers. Trips should be carefully planned, however, with learning objectives and a list of questions and issues for discussion raised in advance. This will help to prevent workers returning simply with lasting impressions of the furnishings and physical layout of the agency rather than an understanding of its operational goals and procedures!

5. *Financing membership of professional societies*. This may provide opportunities to keep abreast of new developments, to meet new colleagues and to discover if local support groups exist.

6. *Investigating college courses*. Colleges of adult education, univer-

sities, and polytechnics may offer (or be persuaded to offer) relevant training programmes that workers can either attend in their own time or negotiate a period of release from normal work responsibilities.

7. *Facilitating attendance at professional conferences, seminars, and conventions.* The benefits can be maximized by asking workers to report back to colleagues and management on their return.

Where to get further information

Sources of information on training related to alcohol use and misuse will vary from profession to profession and from country to country. As a general guide, it is hoped that the following suggestions will prove helpful.

Local sources	In-house training departments
	Nurse training schemes
	Postgraduate medical centres
	Specialist agencies
	Voluntary organizations
	Health-education/promotion units
	Universities, polytechnics, colleges
Regional sources	Regional-based specialist services
	Regional Health Authority training departments
	Regional Health Promotion services
National sources	National agencies providing alcohol services
	National specialist trainers' groups
	Special projects including research projects
	Nationally recognized centres of excellence
	Professional colleges or societies
	National voluntary organizations

It could also be worthwhile becoming a member of a specialist voluntary organization and/or subscribing regularly to a specialist journal or publication.

Glossary of terms

Alcohol or alcohol-related problems. A range of problems — physical, psychological, legal, economic — arising from the inappropriate use of alcohol. May affect the individual and/or spouse/partner, family, friends, employer.

BAL. Blood-alcohol level, the concentration of alcohol in the blood.

Cognitive skills. Mental abilities related to knowledge and perception.

Collusion. Secret agreement, co-operation with, or acceptance of drinking behaviour.

Delirium tremens. A form of delirium with tremors and frightening delusions associated with cessation of heavy, long-term alcohol consumption.

Depressant/drug effect. The depressant effect of alcohol on the body's central nervous system. May alter the way the body functions and/or an individual's behaviour and/or an individual's emotional state.

Fermentation. The process by which certain yeasts convert the carbon, hydrogen, and oxygen of sugar and water into ethyl alcohol and carbon dioxide.

Foetal alcohol syndrome (FAS). A set of varying characteristics observed in newly born children of heavy-drinking women. May include physical and/or mental defects.

Game playing. A form of communication that is neither open nor honest. It includes a series of transactions between players, an ulterior motive (often not stated) and a positive/negative payoff for one or more players.

Heavy drinking. The level of alcohol consumption associated with acute problems such as accidents, gastritis, weight fluctuation, hangovers, nausea, diarrhoea. May also lead to chronic, long-term problems and physical and or psychological dependence.

Intoxication. A state in which the drug effects of alcohol are experienced.

Metabolization. The process by which the body converts alcohol into energy. Unused energy may be stored as fat.

Model. A simplified, theoretical framework used to explain and illustrate complex concepts and processes.

Moderate drinking. A non-harmful level of drinking appropriate to the age, sex, health, and circumstances of the individual.

Mortality rate. The rate of alcohol-induced deaths.

Payoffs. Perceived rewards (physical, mental, social) from carrying out certain actions.

Physical dependence. The condition that develops when alcohol consumption causes physical changes in the body so that it can only function smoothly when alcohol is present. If alcohol is not present, the drinker may experience physical withdrawal symptoms such as nausea, shaking, and sweating. If the drinker takes a further drink to avoid these symptoms, he is said to be physically dependent on alcohol.

Physiological effects. The physical effects of alcohol on living tissues and organs of the human body.

Problem drinker. An individual whose inappropriate alcohol consumption causes him to experience one or more alcohol or alcohol-related problems.

Prohibition. Legislation introduced in America in 1920, which outlawed the manufacture, sale, and transportation (but not the possession) of domestic and foreign liquor within the United States.

Psychological dependence. A strong desire for the effects that alcohol provides and/or the life style, role, or activities associated with drinking. When the drinker experiences strong negative feelings in the absence of alcohol and the life style, role, or activities associated with it, he is said to be psychologically dependent. There are degrees of dependence and dependence does not always cause problems.

Psychotropic. Mind-altering, alters the level of consciousness.

Rehabilitation. Process which aims to enable the individual to lead as independent and fulfilling a life as possible in the community.

Relapse. The return to previous (usually undesirable) ways of coping with or reacting to a situation. For example, a return to heavy drinking after a period of abstinence or controlled drinking.

Relief drinking. The practice of drinking alcohol to relieve or ward off apparent or potential ill-effects of previous (heavy) alcohol consumption.

Socialization. The process of learning or being trained to function as an acceptable member of society.

Teetotal. An adjective describing someone who never drinks alcohol.

Tolerance. The cumulative process by which the body adapts to the repeated presence of alcohol and builds up a resistance to it. Greater doses are needed to achieve and maintain the original effect.

Topping-up effect. The process that raises the blood-alcohol level by drinking more alcohol before the body has had time to metabolize alcohol previously consumed. May lead to accidents when an individual misunderstands or fails to recognize how intoxicated he is.

Transactional analysis. A system incorporating knowledge and skills used to analyse communications between individuals.

Units. The standard measurement applied to all types of alcoholic drinks, used to measure consumption (see Figure 7.1).

Recommended reading

Alcohol Concern (ed) (1987) *Teaching about Alcohol Problems*, Woodhead-Faulkner, Cambridge.

Camberwell Council on Alcoholism (1980) *Women and Alcohol*, Tavistock, London.

Ewles, L. and Simnett, I. (1985) *Promoting Health. A Practical Guide to Health Education*, Wiley and Sons, Chichester.

Grant, M. and Gwinner, P. (eds) (1979) *Alcoholism in Perspective*, Croom Helm, London.

Heather, N. and Robertson, I. (1983) *Controlled Drinking*, Methuen, London.

Heather, N., Robertson, I., and Davies, T. (eds) (1985) *The Misuse of Alcohol: Crucial Issues in Dependence, Treatment and Prevention*, Croom Helm, London.

McConville, B. (1983) *Women under the Influence. Alcohol and its Impact*, Virago Press, London.

Meyer, M. (1982) *Drinking Problems equal Family Problems*, Momenta, Lancaster.

Munro, E.A., Manthei, R.J., and Small, J.J. (1983) *Counselling. A Skills Approach*, Methuen, New Zealand.

Orford, J. (1985) *Excessive Appetites: A Psychological View of Addictions*, Wiley and Sons, Chichester.

Orford, J. and Harwin, J. (eds) (1982) *Alcohol and the Family*, Croom Helm, London.

Plant, M.A. (ed) (1982) *Drinking and Problem Drinking*, Junction Books, London.

Robertson, I. and Heather, N. (1986) *Let's drink to your health! A self-help guide to sensible drinking*, British Psychological Society, Leicester.

Robinson, D. and Tether, P. (1986) *Preventing Alcohol Problems*, Associated Book Publishers, London.

Royal College of Psychiatrists (1986) *Alcohol: Our Favourite Drug*, Tavistock Publications, London.

Bibliography

Albretson, C.S. and Vaglum, P. (1979) 'The alcoholic's wife and her conflicting-roles', in D. Robinson, (ed.) *Alcohol Problems, Reviews, Research and Recommendations*, Macmillan Press.

Alcoholics Anonymous (1955) Alcoholics Anonymous Publishing Company, New York.

Berne, E. (1964) *Games People Play*, Grove Press, New York.

Berne, E. (1973) *What do you say after you say hello?* Grove Press, New York.

Bethune, H. (1985) *Off the Hook. Coping with Addiction*, Methuen Children's Books Ltd., London.

Bobbe, R.A. and Schaffer, R.H. (1968) 'Mastering change: breakthrough projects and beyond', *American Management Association Bulletin*, New York (120), p. 7.

Brandes, D. and Ginnis, P. (1986) *A Guide to Student-Centred Learning*, Basil Blackwell, Oxford pp. 20–1, 85.

Cartwright, A. (1985) 'Is treatment an effective way of helping clients resolve difficulties associated with alcohol? in N. Heather, I. Robertson, and P. Davies (eds), *The Misuse of Alcohol: Crucial Issues in Dependence, Treatment and Prevention*, Croom Helm, London and Sydney, pp. 123, 124–7, 131–3.

Clements, R. (1980) *A Guide to Transactional Analysis. A Handbook for Managers and Trainers*, Insight Training Limited, London, p. 36.

Clare, A.W. (1979) 'The Causes of Alcoholism', in M. Grant and P. Gwinner (eds), *Alcoholism in Perspective*, Croom Helm, London pp. 64–76.

Cork, R.M. (1969) *The Forgotten Children. A Study of Children with Alcoholic Parents*, Alcoholism and Drug Research Foundation of Ontario, Toronto.

Cotton, N.S. (1979) 'The familial Incidence of Alcoholism: A Review', *Journal of Studies on Alcohol, 40*, 89–116.

Davies, D.L. (1979) 'Services for alcoholics', in M. Grant and P. Gwinner (eds), *Alcoholism in Perspective*, Croom Helm, London, pp. 109–10.

Denney, R.C. (1986) *Alcohol and Accidents*, Sigma, Wilmslow, Cheshire, pp. 62–6.

Dewey, J. (ed.) (1916) 'Experience and thinking' in *Democracy and Education*, Macmillan, New York.

Dowdell, P. (1981) 'Alcohol and pregnancy. A review of the literature 1966–80',

Nursing Times, 21 October, 1981.

Egan, G. (1985) *Exercises in Helping Skills*, Brooks Cole Publishing Company, Belmont, California, pp. 59–60.

Egan, G. (1986) *The Skilled Helper. A Systematic Approach to Effective Helping*, Brooks Cole Publishing Company, Belmont, California, pp. 26, 41, 149–52, 162–9, 248, 325–6.

Ewles, L. and Simnett, I. (1985) *Promoting Health: A Practical Guide to Health Education*, John Wiley and Sons, Chichester, p. 20, 30, 52–3, 93.

Fishbein, M. and Ajzen, I. (1975) *Belief, Attitude, Intention and Behaviour. An Introduction to Theory and Research* Addison Wesley, USA and Canada, p. 131.

Glassner, B. and Loughlin, B. (1987) *Drugs in Adolescent Worlds. Burnouts to Straights*, Macmillan Press, London, p. 199.

Grant, M. (1979) Prevention, in M. Grant and P. Gwinner (eds) *Alcoholism in Perspective*, Croom Helm, London, p. 90–1.

Grant, M. (1982) 'Prevention', in M. Plant, (ed.) *Drinking and Problem Drinking*, Junction Books, London, p. 181.

Grant, M. and Gwinner, P. (1979) *Alcoholism in Perspective*, Croom Helm, London, pp. 42–3.

Gwinner, P. (1979) 'Treatment approaches', in M. Grant and P. Gwinner (eds), *Alcoholism in Perspective*, Croom Helm, London, p. 115.

Hansen, A. (1986) 'The portrayal of alcohol on television', *Health Education Journal, 45*, 3, 127.

Harwin, J. and Hunt, L. (1979) 'Working with alcoholics', in M. Grant and P. Gwinner (eds), *Alcoholism in Perspective*, Croom Helm, London, pp. 135, 143–51.

Health Education Council (1986) *That's the Limit! A Guide to Sensible Drinking*, Health Education Council, London, p. 9.

Henley, A. (1979) *Asian Patients in Hoispital and at Home*, King Edward's Hospital Fund, London, Chapter 12.

Howe, B. and Wright, L. (1987) *Drugs: Responding to the Challenge*, Health Education Authority, London, pp. 112–22, 158, 173–84.

NIAAA (1981) *Information and Feature Service*, National Institute on Alcohol Abuse and Alcoholism, *84*, 6, June.

Janzen, C. (1977) 'Families in the treatment of alcoholism', *Journal of Studies on Alcohol, 38*, 114–30.

Karpman, S.B. (1969) 'Fairy tales and script drama analysis', *Transactional Analysis Bulletin, 7*, (26), 39, April.

Laird, D. (1985) *Approaches to Training and Development*, Addison-Wesley Publishing Company, USA and Canada, pp. 60–2.

Lawrence, T. and Cran, J. (1987) 'Alcohol and the Family – roles, patterns and responses in family relationships where one or more members has an alcohol problem', in Alcohol Concern (eds) *Teaching about Alcohol Problems*, Woodhead Faulkener, Cambridge, pp. 63–73.

Lawson, W. (1900) Alliance News, United Kingdom Temperance Alliance, p. 779.

Malan, D.H. (1963) *A study of brief psychotherapy*, Tavistock, London.

Maslow, A.H. (1943) 'A Theory of human motivations', *Psychological Review*,

50, 370–96.

McConville, B. (1983) *Women under the Influence. Alcohol and its Impact*, Virago Press, London, pp. 84, 96.

McKechnie, R. (1985) 'Alcohol, contexts and undesirable consequences: what is to be prevented?, In N. Heather, I. Robertson, and P. Davies (eds), *The Misuse of Alcohol: Crucial Issues in Dependence, Treatment and Prevention*, Croom Helm, London pp. 197–213.

Meyer, M. (1982) *Drinking Problems equal Family Problems: Practical Guidelines for the Problem Drinker, the Partner and all those involved*, Momenta, Lancaster.

Munro, E.A., Manthei, R.J and Small, J.J. (1983) *Counselling: A Skills Approach*, Methuen, New Zealand, p. 56.

Orford, J. (1979) 'Alcohol and the Family', in M. Grant and P. Gwinner (eds) *Alcoholism in Perspective*, Croom Helm, London, p. 88.

Orford, J. (1987) 'Alcohol problems and the family', in T. Heller, M. Gott, and C. Jeffrey (eds), *Drug Use and Misuse*, Open University, Milton Keynes and Wiley and Sons, Chichester, pp. 76–81.

Orford, J., Guthrie, S., Nicholls, P., Oppenheimer, E., Egert, S., and Hensman, C. (1975) 'Self-reported coping behaviour of wives of alcoholics and its associations with drinking outcome', *Journal of Studies on Alcohol 36*, 1254–67.

Orford, J., Oppenheimer, E., Egert, S., Hensman, C., and Guthrie, S. (1976) 'The cohesiveness of alcoholism. Complicated marriages and its influence on treatment outcome', *British Journal of Psychiatry, 128*, 318–39.

Prochaska, J.O. and Di Clemente, C.C. (1982) 'Transtheoretical therapy toward a more integrated model of change', *Psychotherapy: Theory, Research and Practice, 19*, 276–88.

Prochaska, J.O. and Di Clemente, C.C. (1983) 'Stages and processes of self-change of smoking: toward an integrated model of change', *Journal of Consulting Clinical Psychology, 51*, 390–5.

Raistrick, D. and Davidson, J.R. (1987) 'Treatment and Change', in T. Heller, M. Gott and C. Jeffrey (eds) *Drug Use and Misuse*, Wiley and Sons, Chichester, and The Open University, Milton Keynes, p. 146.

Rapoport, L. (1965) 'State of crisis: some theoretical considerations', in H.J. Parad (ed.) *Crisis Intervention*, Family Service Association of America, New York.

Redl, F. (1966) *When we deal with children*, Free Press, New York, p. 216.

Reich, B. and Adcock, C. (1976) Values, Attitudes and Behaviour Change, Methuen, London.

Riordan, R.J. Matheny, K.B., and Harris, C.W. (1978) 'Helping counselors minimize reluctance', *Counselor Education and Supervision, 18*, 6–13.

Ripple, L. (1964) *Motivation, Capacity and Opportunity*, University of Chicago Press, Chicago.

Robertson, I. and Heather, N. (1986) *Let's drink to your health! A self-help guide to sensible drinking*, British Psychological Society, pp. 19, 64–5.

Robertson, I., Hodgson, H., Orford, J. *et al.* (1984) *Psychology and Problem Drinking*, British Psychological Society, Leicester.

Royal College of General Practitioners (1986) *Alcohol — A Balanced View*, Royal

College of General Practitioners, London, p. 54.

Royal College of Psychiatrists (1986) *Alcohol: Our Favourite Drug. New report on alcohol and alcohol-related problems from a special committee of the RCPS*, Tavistock, London pp. 18, 54, 71–2, 106, 168–9.

Rogers, C. (1961) *On Becoming a Person*, Houghton Mifflin Co., Boston, p. 385.

Schaffer, J.B. and Tyler, J.D. (1979) 'Degree of sobriety in male alcoholics and coping styles used by their wives', *British Journal of Psychiatry, 135* 431–7.

Seixas, J. (1980) *How to Cope with an Alcoholic Parent*, Canongate, Edinburgh.

Simnett, I., Wright, L., and Evans, M. (1983) *Drinking Choices. A Training Manual for Alcohol Educators*, Health Education Council/TACADE, pp. 69, 73–4.

Snell, R. (1987) 'The challenge of painful and unpleasant emotions', in V. Hodgson, S. Mann, and R. Snell (eds), *Beyond Distance Teaching — Towards Open Learning*, Open University Press, Milton Keynes, p. 63.

Steiner, C. (1971) *Games Alcoholics Play*, Grove Press, New York, pp. 11, 82.

Steiner, C. (1979) *Healing Alcoholism*, Grove Press, New York, p. 195.

Steinglass, P. (1982) 'The roles of alcohol in family systems', in J. Orford and J. Harwin (eds), *Alcohol and the Family*, Croom Helm, London.

Sterne, W.S. and Pitman, D.J. (1965) 'The concept of motivation: a source of institutional and professional blockage in the treatment of alcoholics', *Quarterly Journal of Studies on Alcohol, 26*, 44–55.

Streissguth, A. (1979) A lecture reported in *New Scientist*, 11 January.

Stuteville, J.R. (1970) 'Psychic defenses against high fear appeals: A key marketing variable', *Journal of Marketing, 34*, 39–45.

Tones, B.K. (1987) 'Devising strategies for preventing drug misuse: the role of the health action model', *Health Education Research, Theory and Practice, 2*, 4, 305–17.

Truax, C. and Wargo, D. (1966) 'Psychotherapeutic encounters that change behaviour: for better or worse', *American Journal of Psychotherapy, 20*, pp. 499–520.

Turner, C. (1983) *Developing Interpersonal Skills*, Further Education Staff College, Bristol, Chapter 5.

Williams, G.P. and Brake, G.T. (1980) *Drink in Great Britain 1900–1979*, B. Edsall and Co. London, pp. 4–11, 599–601.

Works, D.A. (1974) *New Hope, New Responsibilities*, Washington Department of Transportation, Washington, p. 7.

US Journal of Alcohol and Drug Dependence (1981) 'Worldwide Consumption Continues to Climb', a lecture given by Dr Perry London, *Journal of Alcohol and Drug Dependence, 5* (2), 19, March.

Zimbardo, P., Ebbeson, E., and Maslach, C. (1977) *Influencing Attitudes and Changing Behaviour*, Addison Wesley Publishing Company, USA and Canada, pp. 42, 233.

Index

contexts 18, 52, 66; cultural 97; drinking 31-2; family 93, 134
contraception *see* women
contracts, setting 54, 64
coping strategies 20, 48, 67, 150; alternative 73; discovering 156; extending 155; family 118, 125-7; in relapse 152; wives' 128-30
crisis 48; professionally provoked 161; relapse 152-7

danger spots 56
decision-taking 61, 78, 148; balance sheet 137; client involvement 152; models 27-31; strategies 132
denial 84, 149
dependence 6-8, 10, 43, 63, 100
Drinker's diary 68, 81, 88, 109-11; self-monitoring 133 *see also* monitoring
drink/driving 105-6
Drinkwatchers 67
drugs and alcohol 108-9
drug effect 10, 35-6, 56

education 19-20; aims and objectives 21-2 *see also* alcohol education needs, approaches; caring activity 72-3; exercises 109-16, 134-40; in workload 46, 48; techniques 79-80; value 148 *see also* evaluation
Egan G. 96, 131-3, 149-51, 155
emotional pain 143-4, 155-8; barrier 146
empowering, clients 20, 48, 144-5, 156 *see also* education in workload
evaluation, alcohol education 74; planning 80-3; questionnaire 82
eye contact 87-8

factual information 39, 147; for families 130; need for 96-7
family 10, 36-9, 46-8, 147; alcohol

education 20, 65, 118 *see also* alcohol education exercises; ethnic 146; functioning 117-19, 122, 127 *see also* games; system 155 *see also* coping strategies, models
feedback, giving and receiving 94-5; on progress 152 *see also* evaluation
foetal alcohol syndrome (FAS) *see* pregnancy
focusing 120-1, 126-7; exercises 137-40; principles 155-7

games 20, 36-9, 131; analysing 124-5 *see also* family functioning
goals 54-6, 62, 69, 151; achieving 96-7; behaviour 63-4, 68; setting 74, 77-9, 133, 150
groupwork *see* skills

hangovers 10, 34-5, 46; cures 41
harm, alcohol-related 15, 20, 40, 50-1, 62; minimising 46, 67-9, 97-100 *see also* monitoring units
heavy drinking 11-15, 49, 52, 93, 152; in pregnancy 107-8; male 32-41
helping processes 45, 96, 133, 150-2

intervention 13, 43-6, 50; skills 17-22; unwelcome 39

Karpman triangle 123-5 *see also* transactional analysis

licensing laws 4, 17
low/non-alcoholic drinks 49, 67 *see also* calorie counting, controlling consumption

marriage 119-20
Maslow, A.H. 30-1
media 10, 33-4, 46
menstrual cycle *see* women
models 5-8; family 117-19; of